EXTREME

FAITH

Tapping God's Power

BOB RUSSELL

With Rusty Russell

Standard
PUBLISHING
CINCINNATI, OHIO

All Scripture quotations, unless otherwise indicated, are taken from the HOLY
BIBLE, NEW INTERNATIONAL VERSION®. NIV®.
Copyright ©1973, 1978, 1984 by International Bible Society.
Used by permission of Zondervan Publishing House.
All rights reserved.

ISBN 0-7847-7101-4

Edited by Lynn Perrigo
Cover design by DesignTeam

Published by Standard Publishing, Cincinnati, Ohio
A division of Standex International Corporation
© 2002 by Robert L. Russell and Robert L. Russell, Jr.
All rights reserved
Printed in the United States of America

Contents

INTRODUCTION

The Untapped Power

One of my mentors in the ministry, Olin Hay, often told about a contrasting sight he saw while traveling through the mountains of east Tennessee years ago. He saw a series of powerful electrical lines that gracefully swooped down within a few feet of a small cabin nestled against the side of a steep hill. As he drove by in the early evening, he could see the flicker of an oil lamp in the window of the cabin and realized there was no electricity in the house. A tremendous power source hanging within feet of the cabin wasn't being tapped.

Brother Hay used that scene to illustrate the lack of power in the lives of most Christians. God has promised us that all the power of heaven is available to those who trust in Him, but most of us don't tap into that power. Our Christian testimonies are just a flicker of what they could be.

Throughout His Word, God promises to empower those who live by faith:

"If you have faith as small as a mustard seed, you can say to this mountain, 'Move from here to there' and it will move. Nothing will be impossible for you" (Matthew 17:20).

"And without faith it is impossible to please God, because anyone who comes to him must believe that he exists and that he rewards those who earnestly seek him" (Hebrews 11:6).

"For everyone born of God overcomes the world. This is the victory that has overcome the world, even our faith" (1 John 5:4).

God wants us to move mountains, win victories, overcome fear, inspire others, and endure trials. God has promised incredible power to those who really trust in Him, but that potential virtually goes untapped. It just sits there, waiting to be used, because we lack faith.

I'm convinced that every Christian wants more faith. Most of us believe God's promises are true, but when we are tested, we discover our faith is weak. We doubt. We question. We delay. We play it safe. Like the disciples, we pray, "Lord increase our faith!" Like the father who wanted Jesus to heal his son, we plead, "Lord, I believe. Help my unbelief."

How do we get more faith? Try harder? Pray for it? Wish for it? Faith is increased in two practical ways.

Read About People of Faith

Reading about people of faith in God's Word increases our faith. "Faith comes from hearing the message, and the message is heard through the word of Christ" (Romans 10:17).

The more times we observe a plane landing safely, the more we believe it will do so again and the less we fear getting on board. The more we see how God kept His promises with imperfect Bible characters, the more we believe His Word will prove true in our lives. When we see God keeping His promises again and again, we're more likely to believe He will do the same for us.

Act on the Faith You Have

It's not enough to just read about people of faith. Your faith can be increased by simply acting on the faith you have. James said, "Faith without deeds is useless" (James 2:20). You learn to play baseball by playing baseball. You learn to play the piano by playing the piano. You learn to overcome the fear of flying by flying. You learn to walk by faith by walking by faith. God always blesses those who "walk by faith, not by sight" (2 Corinthians 5:7, *KJV*).

Four years ago, I received a disturbing phone call that my father, who had been completely healthy, had suffered a serious stroke and might not live. I was stunned by the news. I had a deep love for my father, who was my biggest fan. When I received the call, I was in Florida preparing to speak for a seniors' conference in just a matter of hours. I wondered what I should do. Should I cancel the speaking engagement? Would I be able to concentrate if I tried to speak? Would I be able to function at all since I was so worried about my dad?

I shared the news with a lifelong friend and fellow preacher, Bill Gaslin, and asked him what I should do. Bill sympathized with me for a moment and then said, "Well, now it's time for you to believe what you say you believe." That wasn't crass. It was what I needed to hear. Was my faith just mental agreement that God's Word is true, or was I willing to walk by faith? Would I trust that God would care for my father in his time of need and provide strength for me in my time of weakness? Would I believe and act on the promise that "in all things God works for the good of those who love him" (Romans 8:28) and allow others to see my assurance in Christ? Or would I fall apart and whine about God's unfairness?

I spoke for the convention. I asked the fellow believers to pray for my family and me during a difficult time. And the Lord was true to His promise that He will not allow anyone to endure more than he can bear (1 Corinthians 10:13).

My father passed away a few days later. Throughout the difficult days and times of grief that followed, I remembered Bill's words to me: "Now it's time for you to believe what you say you believe." I've continued ministering to others because I believe the promises of God—that He will comfort the brokenhearted and resurrect the dead.

This book is written to help you increase your faith. In Hebrews 11, the Hebrew writer gives us his list of heroes—a list of people who exhibited their faith by their actions. One of the reasons that list inspires me is that they were normal people. In fact, there were times when they made some stupid decisions, did some horrible things, and even had serious *lapses* in faith. If these people are the "heroes of faith," then there is hope for all of us! I love what Max Lucado wrote:

> They aren't exactly what you'd call a list of "Who's Who in Purity and Sainthood." In fact, some of their antics and attitudes would make you think of the Saturday night crowd at the county jail. What few halos there are among this befuddled bunch could probably use a bit of straightening and polish. Yet, strange as it may seem it is this very humanness that makes these people refreshing. . . . If you ever wonder how in the world God could use you to change the world, look at these people. . . . The reassuring lesson is clear. God used (and uses!) people to change the world. *People!* Not saints or superhumans or geniuses, but people. Crooks, creeps, lovers, and liars—he uses them all.[1]

By studying these scriptural characters who stepped out in bold faith, I hope you'll be inspired and instructed that God always keeps His Word. He'll do what He says He will do.

The next step of action is up to you. When you are finished with this study, take a risk of faith. God is looking for people who will keep climbing, persevering, and believing no matter what. He doesn't need talented people, beautiful people, or intelligent people; He just needs people who will have faith. He needs people who—when life is difficult, when God calls and His commands don't make sense, when our sense of security tempts us to camp out, when giants intimidate us, when people let us down, and when the road just gets long—will act on their mustard seed-sized faith and reach up to the power source that is just above them.

Put God to the test and see that His promises are true. Plant the mustard seed. You'll discover your faith will increase. Your confidence in God's promises will mature. Your Christian life will be empowered by a constant flow of God's Holy Spirit in you. "With this in mind, we constantly pray for you, that our God may count you worthy of his calling, and that by his power he may fulfill every good purpose of yours and every act prompted by your faith" (2 Thessalonians 1:11).

1

ABRAHAM:
When God's Promises
Seem Impossible,

Faith Trusts

Hebrews 11:8-19; Genesis 12:1-9; 18:1-3, 9-14; 21:1-6; 22:1-14

Years ago, Isaiah Moore, a professor at the College of the Scriptures in Louisville, decided that he would remarry when he was widowed for the fifth time at age eighty-nine. Wayne Smith, the renowned preacher from Lexington, Kentucky, asked him why he was marrying again at that age. Professor Moore quipped, "I've always wanted to have a son." He even bought a new house close to an elementary school. Wayne Smith said, "Brother Moore, you ought to be the president of the Optimist Club!"

God made a bold promise to Abraham: "I will make you into a great nation and I will bless you" (Genesis 12:2). That promise seemed impossible to believe because Abraham's wife, Sarah, had never had a child—and she was sixty-five years old! Abraham himself was seventy-five years old at the time he received this promise, and it would be twenty-five years before the promise was fulfilled.

> Against all hope, Abraham in hope believed and so became the father of many nations, just as it had been said to him, "So shall your offspring be." Without weakening in his faith, he faced the fact that his body was as good as dead—since he was about a hundred years old—and that Sarah's womb was also dead. Yet he did not waver through unbelief regarding the promise of God, but was strengthened in his faith and

gave glory to God, being fully persuaded that God had power
to do what he had promised (Romans 4:19-21).

Abraham Trusted God's Provision When He Was Called to Move

The LORD had said to Abram, "Leave your country, your
people and your father's household and go to the land I will
show you." . . . So Abram left, as the LORD had told him;
and Lot went with him. Abram was seventy-five years old
when he set out from Haran (Genesis 12:1, 4).

It's always difficult to move, but some moves are more difficult
than others. Abraham's move was challenging for several reasons.

Abraham had many possessions. Abraham was a wealthy man
with many cattle and possessions. I remember the first time my
wife and I moved. A few days before we were married, four friends
from college helped me move Judy's belongings from her second-
story apartment to the house we would be renting. She had a new
Wurlitzer spinet piano. The movers had said, "We're not going to
take that piano down those narrow steps." So four of us lugged it
down the steps, onto the truck, and into the house. I thought we
had moved it without a scratch. We felt so good about it. But
when Judy walked into the room, she looked at it from fifteen feet
away and said, "Oh Bob, look what you did to my piano!" Sure
enough, just under the bottom of the keyboard was a two-inch-
long scratch. Thankfully, our marriage survived that scratch on her
beautiful piano, but we learned not to move very often. Moving is
risky! Abraham was taking all his possessions with him in a day
when there was no movers' insurance to cover damages.

Abraham was an old man. Abraham was already seventy-five
years old. It's much more difficult to uproot after that many years
in one place. My wife and I had enough difficulty moving when

we were in our twenties. We've only moved once since those early years—when we were in our forties—to a new home less than five miles away. By that time, we had accumulated a lot more stuff and had two children to consider. We also had neighbors we were leaving behind whom we had known for twenty years. It was a very difficult move even though we were not even leaving town.

Abraham was leaving a cultured area. J. Oswald Sanders reported on some archaeologists' discovery of a tablet in the area of Ur of the Chaldeans. The tablet revealed that the mathematicians of Ur were engaged in finding the solution to a trigonometry problem that continues to intrigue mathematicians today. Abraham was leaving an advanced culture. Ur was the center of trade in that day. It would be the equivalent of someone leaving Chicago or New York to wander through the plains, not knowing where the next civilized town would be.

Abraham was taking his extended family with him. Abraham's father, nephew, and their families accompanied Abraham on this move. Abraham felt responsible for them and their children. And all of them had possessions, as well as servants and their families. It's difficult to travel somewhere with two children in the backseat of a car. Imagine traveling in such a large caravan! Not only did Abraham feel responsible for all of them, but the pace at which they traveled must have been unbearably slow.

Abraham didn't know where he was going. This had to have been the most difficult part of the move. Imagine breaking the news to your wife that the family will be moving. She asks the natural question, "Where are we going?" And you say, "I don't know, but God has told me to move, so we're leaving." What would your wife say? "You've gotta be kidding!"

As one preacher said, "True faith is content to travel under sealed orders." The writer of Hebrews said, "By faith Abraham, when called to go to a place he would later receive as his inheritance, obeyed and went, even though he did not know where he was going" (Hebrews 11:8).

Abraham trusted that God was not confined to one place, but that God would go with him wherever he went and provide everything he needed.

About fifteen years ago, I attended the Praise Gathering in Indianapolis and listened to Tony Campolo issue the most dramatic call for missionary recruits that I've ever heard. With ten thousand people listening, he chose to focus on the young people in the audience who would soon be making career decisions. He said:

> I want to talk with you college students out there. What are you going to do with your life? Are you going to become a schoolteacher? Kids, to be honest, we have more schoolteachers right now than we need. People with master's degrees in education can't find jobs. Are you going to become a doctor? Most American cities don't have a need for doctors. Medical schools have a long waiting list. Are you going to become a lawyer? We sure don't need more lawyers!
>
> Young people, I'm going to tell you the truth: America doesn't need you. But Haiti needs you. Indonesia needs you. Third world countries need teachers and doctors and lawyers. Jesus Christ needs you to obey His command to go into all the world and preach the gospel.
>
> So tonight I'm going to offer a call to college students to come forward and say to Jesus Christ, "I will obey your command to go into a world where I'm needed. I will give up all the comforts of home and dedicate my life to go to a third world country where my life can count." If you're willing to make that decision tonight, I'm going to ask that you come forward right now. We're not going to sing "Just as I Am" or any of that stuff. I'm not going to ask people to bow their heads and close their eyes. If you come forward, I want people to stare at you. Jesus calls us to live a life of courage and testimony. Right now, if you're willing to give your life to missions, if you feel God's call, come forward as we wait in absolute silence.

You could have heard a pin drop. Two thoughts ran through my mind. First, I thought no one would go forward. I was wrong. Scores of college students flocked to the platform. Campolo said, "Now I want to talk to you fat cats out there. You know—you guys who are making a hundred thousand a year and socking it away. These kids need someone to finance their way. If God is laying it on your heart to bankroll them, you come forward." A few did come forward, although the college students far outnumbered the "fat cats" who committed to help them.

The second thought that ran through my mind was that none of those students would truly follow through with their decisions. They had made an emotional commitment and when the emotions wore off, they would forget their decisions. However, while I was on a trip to Africa, I ate dinner one evening with Tim and Marcia Ross, missionaries to the Maasai in Kenya. I asked them how they decided to enter missions. Tim said, "I was at the Praise Gathering in Indianapolis years ago, and Tony Campolo issued a call for recruits to third world countries. I felt God leading me, so I went forward."

Tim's wife interrupted. "I sat there and watched him go. I thought, 'Oh, no!' I didn't want to leave home and go to Africa. But that's what Tim believed God wanted him to do, so I followed him here. And God has been faithful."

Abraham Trusted God's Power When He Was Called to Sacrifice

Some time later God tested Abraham. He said to him, "Abraham!" "Here I am," he replied. Then God said, "Take your son, your only son, Isaac, whom you love, and go to the region of Moriah. Sacrifice him there as a burnt offering on one of the mountains I will tell you about" (Genesis 22:1, 2).

An unreasonable command

Abraham must have been stunned by what appeared to be a most unreasonable command. God had promised Abraham that there would be many descendants through his son Isaac. How could that happen if Isaac was dead? The pagan nations around him practiced human sacrifice, but Abraham knew that was not God's will. Had God changed His mind? Was He not a good and gracious deity after all? Abraham loved Isaac with all his heart. How could God ask this of him?

I have two sons who are now grown with children of their own. It was hard to give them up to marriage even though I loved the girls they were marrying. (Since then, I've discovered I've gained much more than I gave up!) I remember when my son Phil got married. Before the ceremony, he was a little nervous. Not only was this one of the most important days of his life, but the '63 Corvette he had borrowed to drive away from the church had broken down on the way to the church and he almost didn't make it to the wedding. He asked, "Dad, will you pray with me?" I could tell he needed it.

The ceremony was beautiful. Both Phil and Lisa were enthusiastic and happy. As I was winding down my remarks and fighting back my emotions, I said, "Phil, you've seen a plaque in your grandparents' home that reads, 'Jesus is the head of this house.'" I looked up and saw tears streaming down his cheeks. My voice started to crack and I began to cave in. He sniffled. I swallowed hard. He sniffed his way through the vows and I wondered if we'd make it.

Then I said, "Will you take this ring?" He turned to take the ring from Andy Dabney, his best man. Andy began to pretend to search for the ring and all the groomsmen followed suit. The congregation burst into laughter because not only was it funny, but we all needed the comic relief. While everyone was laughing, I looked at Phil and he whispered, "I love you, Dad." I was a basket case and I'm not sure how I made it through the rest of that ceremony.

Can you imagine hearing God say to Abraham, "I want you to sacrifice your own son, the son whom you love, on the altar"? I would have expected Abraham to immediately protest, "No way! You can't ask that of me. That's completely beyond reason, Lord!" But Abraham obeyed unconditionally.

Abraham's unconditional obedience

> Early the next morning Abraham got up and saddled his donkey. He took with him two of his servants and his son Isaac. When he had cut enough wood for the burnt offering, he set out for the place God had told him about (Genesis 22:3).

Abraham didn't delay. He didn't beg for more time or wait for a second notice from God. Apparently, Abraham didn't even explain to the boy's mother what was about to happen. He just obeyed.

> On the third day Abraham looked up and saw the place in the distance. He said to his servants, "Stay here with the donkey while I and the boy go over there. We will worship and then we will come back to you" (Genesis 22:4, 5).

We think of worship as singing songs, praying, taking communion, and listening to a sermon. However, ultimate worship is sacrificing ourselves completely to the will of God. Abraham wasn't going to a worship service; he was going to surrender his most precious possession to God. Paul said in Romans, "I urge you, brothers, . . . to offer your bodies as living sacrifices, holy and pleasing to God—this is your spiritual act of worship" (Romans 12:1). The most worshipful thing we can do is to surrender ourselves to God.

Abraham told the servant, "We will worship and then *we* will come back." He wasn't lying. Abraham's faith and trust in God had grown so strong through years of experience that Abraham believed God would keep His promise. God would make sure Isaac was not eliminated because He had promised that through Isaac there would be descendants. As the writer of Hebrews explains,

> By faith Abraham, when God tested him, offered Isaac as a sacrifice. He who had received the promises was about to sacrifice his one and only son, even though God had said to him, "It is through Isaac that your offspring will be reckoned." Abraham reasoned that God could raise the dead, and figuratively speaking, he did receive Isaac back from death (Hebrews 11:17-19).

Abraham was so sure of God's promise that he believed God would raise Isaac from the dead to make it happen.

> Abraham took the wood for the burnt offering and placed it on his son Isaac, and he himself carried the fire and the knife. As the two of them went on together, Isaac spoke up and said to his father Abraham, "Father?" "Yes, my son?" Abraham replied. "The fire and wood are here," Isaac said, "but where is the lamb for the burnt offering?" Abraham answered, "God himself will provide the lamb for the burnt offering, my son." And the two of them went on together (Genesis 22:6-8).

Abraham must have been choking back the tears. It was an extremely tense time for him. Yet even at this point, he still believed God would provide an escape. "God himself will provide the lamb," he told Isaac.

> When they reached the place God had told him about, Abraham built an altar there and arranged the wood on it. He bound his son Isaac and laid him on the altar, on top of the wood (Genesis 22:9).

Most commentators believe that Isaac was between thirteen and thirty years old at this time. He was a strong young man, and

Abraham was very old. Apparently, Isaac did not resist Abraham. He shared his father's faith and believed Abraham knew what was best. Isaac was a type of Christ in this way. Years later, the Son of God would say, "No one takes [my life] from me, but I lay it down of my own accord. I have authority to lay it down and authority to take it up again. This command I received from my Father" (John 10:18). Isaac permitted his father to tie him up and place him on the altar.

"Then [Abraham] reached out his hand and took the knife to slay his son" (Genesis 22:10). Abraham must have been quivering with fear. He had to be sobbing, pleading with God to restrain his hand and begging his son to try to understand. Never before had a loving father or an obedient son been put to such a test as this. Abraham loved his son, but he loved God even more.

An unexpected provision

> But the angel of the LORD called out to him from heaven, "Abraham! Abraham!" "Here I am," he replied. "Do not lay a hand on the boy," he said. "Do not do anything to him. Now I know that you fear God, because you have not withheld from me your son, your only son." Abraham looked up and there in a thicket he saw a ram caught by its horns. He went over and took the ram and sacrificed it as a burnt offering instead of his son (Genesis 22:11-13).

This was an unexpected provision, but there was never a more welcomed interruption of worship! Since Abraham passed the test, God provided a way of escape—a substitute sacrifice. This was the first time that a substitute sacrifice was required, symbolizing what was to come hundreds of years later. As a ram died in Isaac's place, so Jesus would someday die in our place.

An unequivocal blessing

> The angel of the LORD called to Abraham from heaven a second time and said, "I swear by myself, declares the LORD, that because you have done this and have not withheld your son, your only son, I will surely bless you and make your descendants as numerous as the stars in the sky and as the sand on the seashore. Your descendants will take possession of the cities of their enemies, and through your offspring all nations on earth will be blessed, because you have obeyed me" (Genesis 22:15-18).

God promised Abraham that his descendants would be as numerous as the stars of the sky and the sand on the seashore. With the naked eye, man can only count about three thousand stars at the most. For centuries, it seemed like God was making an unscientific comparison when He likened the stars to the sand, but in this day of giant telescopes, we know that such a comparison is very appropriate. When God promised Abraham that he would have many descendants, He wasn't just referring to the Jewish nation, but also to the coming of Jesus Christ and all those who have been grafted into the family of Abraham through Christ. The Bible says, "If you belong to Christ, then you are Abraham's seed, and heirs according to the promise" (Galatians 3:29).

Abraham and Isaac must have descended the mountain filled with exuberance. Once again they had discovered that God is full of grace and truth, and He can be trusted to do what He says He will do.

Have Faith! God Keeps His Word

Someone said, "Faith is going to the end of all the light you have and then taking one more step." God doesn't usually speak to us directly the way He did to Abraham. God partially reveals himself in *creation,* where we see His awesome power, and partially reveals himself in your *conscience,* where you are convicted of sin and encouraged to obey. But God speaks most directly through the person of *Christ.*

Jesus said, "Anyone who has seen me has seen the Father" (John 14:9). Though we can't physically see Jesus, we can see Him by studying His Word. Romans 10:17 says, "Faith comes from hearing the message, and the message is heard through the word of Christ."

Reading great philosophers or listening to skeptics or sitting under the stars in deep thought does not usually increase your faith. You increase your faith by studying the Bible because it reveals God's will. The more you study the Scriptures, the more convinced you become that God keeps seemingly impossible promises:

- God promised Noah that if he built an ark, he would be spared from the flood, and God's word was fulfilled.
- God told Moses that the children of Israel would be delivered out of Egypt and into a land of promise, and God kept His word.
- God promised Joshua that if he would march around Jericho seven times and make a lot of noise, then the city walls would collapse. That didn't seem possible, but God kept His word.
- God told David that he would succeed Saul as king of Israel even though David was only a shepherd boy, and God kept His promise.
- God promised Gideon that with only three hundred men, he would defeat the Midianite hordes, and God's word was true.
- God promised Elijah that it would rain even though there was not a cloud in the sky and there had been no rain for three years, and God kept His word.

- God promised the nation of Israel that He would send forth a redeemer who would save His people from their sins. They waited for centuries, but God fulfilled His promise.
- Jesus promised His disciples that He would die and rise again even though no one had ever come back from the grave on His own power. Jesus kept His word.
- Jesus promised that if His disciples would wait in Jerusalem, they would be filled with power from on high, and the Lord was faithful to His promise.
- Jesus promised that the gates of Hades would not prevail against His church. The church has stood for two thousand years and God has kept His word.

Deuteronomy 7:9 says, "Know therefore that the LORD your God is God; he is the faithful God, keeping his covenant of love to a thousand generations of those who love him and keep his commands." A person of faith trusts that God will keep His promise even though it may seem impossible at the time. Think of some of the promises God has made to us:

God will meet all your needs. "My God will meet all your needs according to his glorious riches in Christ Jesus" (Philippians 4:19). That may seem impossible to you because you have so many unmet needs—needs for companionship, finances, health, peace of mind, understanding. Faith trusts that God will keep His word. He will supply all you need in His time.

God will help you overcome temptation. "No temptation has seized you except what is common to man. And God is faithful; he will not let you be tempted beyond what you can bear. But when you are tempted, he will also provide a way out so that you can stand up under it" (1 Corinthians 10:13). You may endure trials you think are impossible to endure, but faith believes God will keep His word and acts accordingly.

The peace of God will guard your heart. "Do not be anxious about anything, but in everything, by prayer and petition, with thanksgiving, present your requests to God. And the peace of God, which transcends all understanding, will guard your hearts and your minds in Christ Jesus" (Philippians 4:6, 7). We must constantly battle the temptation to worry and stew about the cares of this life and the potential problems of the future. The person of faith who trusts in the providence of God will receive the peace of God.

God will reward tithing. "'Bring the whole tithe into the storehouse, that there may be food in my house. Test me in this,' says the LORD Almighty, 'and see if I will not throw open the floodgates of heaven and pour out so much blessing that you will not have room enough for it'" (Malachi 3:10). You may be down to your last dollar and may not see any way that your resources could increase, but faith believes God will keep His word. He does what we think is impossible.

The earth will endure until Christ returns. "As long as the earth endures, seedtime and harvest, cold and heat, summer and winter, day and night will never cease" (Genesis 8:22). Doom-sayers claim that global warming and the hole in the ozone layer will soon destroy the world. In the late seventies, scientists insisted the earth was getting colder and we would soon have another ice age. Now they're convinced that we have the opposite problem. God promises that His creation will endure until Christ returns, and faith takes comfort in that promise.

The believer will be resurrected. "For my Father's will is that everyone who looks to the Son and believes in him shall have eternal life, and I will raise him up at the last day" (John 6:40). When I visited a Maasai tribe in Kenya, Africa, one of the first Maasai natives I met was a man who looked about ninety years old. He had been coming to the church services but had not become a Christian. I talked to him through an interpreter about Jesus being the Savior, and he nodded. I talked about Jesus forgiving sins, and he agreed. But when I talked about Jesus promising life after death, he turned away with a smirk. He couldn't really believe in the possibility that God would raise him up. That man was living in the most primitive condition imaginable, but he proudly resisted the idea of a resurrection.

Rejecting God's promise has nothing to do with your civility or intelligence. It is a lack of faith. People much less civilized than you or I have rejected Christ, and people much more sophisticated have accepted Christ. Believing in the promise of eternal life is simply a matter of trusting in a God who will keep His word.

Mike Graham was about to become the administrator of Southeast Christian Church. In three months, he was to leave his high-level management position in a large corporation in Chicago, so that he could join our staff in Louisville. That's when Mike discovered he had cancer, and the doctors said he had only six months to live.

However, Mike felt it was God's will to come to Southeast. He believed God still wanted him to make the move even though he was in the midst of painful cancer treatments. He trusted that God would take care of him.

We told Mike to come work for us as long as he could. The elders of our church laid hands on him and prayed for him, asking God to spare his life and use him in ministry. That was twelve years ago, and Mike is still on our staff today! He is still battling cancer, but he's served our church faithfully and has been a tremendous asset. Now we know why God wanted Mike, in the midst of his trial, to move to Louisville. And we're thankful that when God's call was strange and His promise seemed impossible, Mike's faith was strong enough to trust and obey.

2

JOSEPH:
When People Let You Down,
Faith Endures

Hebrews 11:22, 36; Genesis 37:23-36; 39:1-23; 45:1-15

A few months ago, I read an interesting book by Paul Stoltz titled, *Adversity Quotient: Turning Obstacles Into Opportunities*. It's a thought-provoking book that is having a powerful impact on industry and education.

Stoltz's book seeks to answer this question: *Why is it that some people, given equivalent assets and opportunities, succeed where others have failed?* That question takes many forms:

- Why do some organizations thrive on competition while others are crushed?
- Why does one entrepreneur beat unfathomable odds while others give up?
- Why do some parents rear children who are good citizens in neighborhoods riddled with violence and drugs?
- Why does an individual beat the odds, overcoming an abusive childhood, when most don't?
- Why does one inner-city teacher positively impact students' lives while the rest of the faculty barely gets by?
- Why does one laid-off aerospace manager spring to action and reshape her destiny while her counterparts fall into fear and depression?
- Why do so many gifted or high IQ people fall far short of their potential?[2]

For years, the most familiar measure of potential was the IQ test. However, we've learned that while intelligence is an asset, it is by no means the most important determining factor in achievement. Ted Kaczynski, the Unabomber, has a near-genius IQ and the best education. He entered Harvard when he was sixteen years old, graduated when he was twenty, went on to receive a Ph.D. in math from the University of Michigan, and became a tenured professor at the University of California at Berkeley. Yet he quit his teaching position after two years and began living as a hermit. He used his intelligence to kill three people and injure twenty-two others. IQ is not an accurate measurement of a person's potential for success.

More recently, people like Daniel Goleman, author of *Emotional Intelligence,* have attempted to measure a person's EQ, or Emotional Quotient. They claimed that we could better measure a person's chances of success by testing his or her ability to empathize with people, postpone gratification, control impulses, persist, and interact with others. We used to call such characteristics "maturity." EQ remains illusive and difficult to measure.[3]

Stoltz concluded that there is something more important than IQ or EQ in determining success, and that's AQ. Almost all successful people in every field have this one thing in common: They get back up when they fall down. They refuse to quit. They have an amazing resiliency, a high Adversity Quotient.

For example, Thomas Edison was considered a dunce by his grade school teacher, but he was a tenacious inventor. It took him twenty years and fifty thousand experiments to invent a light, durable, efficient battery for use as an independent power supply. Someone said to Edison: "You have failed fifty thousand times. What makes you think you will ever get results?" He replied: "Results? Why, I've gotten a lot of results. I know fifty thousand things that won't work!" Edison had a high AQ. Stoltz says Edison sheds some *light* on the meaning of persistence![4]

Because Stoltz is a mountain climber, he uses the analogy of a group starting up a difficult mountain. When the weather changes and climbing becomes difficult, you can divide people into three categories:

1. *Quitters*—about 20 percent of the people just quit and head back down the mountain.

2. *Campers*—about 60 percent exchange the challenge for security and comfort, and say, "Let's just hunker down right here, set up our tents, settle in, and see if there's a break in the weather."

3. *Climbers*—20 percent keep on going even through adversity.[5]

Stoltz writes:

> Scaling the mountain is an indescribable experience, one only fellow climbers can understand and share. Amid the relief, satisfaction, and exhaustion is a sense of joy and peace as rarefied as the mountain air. Only the climber tastes this sweet success. Those who stay encamped may be justified, as well as warmer and safer, but never will they feel "on purpose" as alive, as proud and as joyful. Success can be defined as the degree to which one moves forward and upward, progressing in one's lifelong mission, despite all obstacles or other forms of adversity.[6]

According to Stoltz, the good news is that while you can't do much to improve your IQ, you can measure and dramatically improve your AQ. You can enhance your ability to take on challenges. To his credit, Stoltz mentions faith as one of the essential root factors for determining your AQ.[7]

One of the most dramatic biblical examples of persistence in spite of adversity is Joseph. He was a man who kept climbing even when people continually let him down. His ability to trust in God despite overwhelming adversity is a reminder of what God can do with someone who has a high AQ and a lot of faith.

Joseph's Family Let Him Down

His mother died

Joseph grew up in a dysfunctional family. Joseph's father, Jacob, had four wives. Joseph's mother, Rachel—his father's favorite wife—died giving birth to her second child, a son named Benjamin. Joseph was just a young boy when his mother died and her death surely had a tremendous impact on him.

My mother had a serious cancer operation when I was in college. I remember being deeply shaken by the incident and praying intensely every day that God would heal her. I'm so thankful God answered those prayers, but I tried to imagine how difficult it would be to go through the death of a parent at a young age. If you've experienced that, you have gone through more adversity than many others.

His father was overindulgent

Joseph was Jacob's favorite son because he was the firstborn son of his favorite wife. Rachel had been barren for many years, so when Joseph came along in Jacob's later years, it was a double blessing. Instead of trying to conceal his favoritism, Jacob showered Joseph with attention and gifts. He even gave him the famous "coat of many colors" of which Joseph's brothers were so envious. Even if you're the favorite child in your family, it's a disadvantage to grow up in a home where all of the children aren't equally loved.

His brothers were abusive

Joseph had ten half-brothers who were extremely jealous of his favored status. Not only were they jealous, but they became hateful and violent. Joseph made the mistake of telling them about a dream he had in which their sheaves of grain all bowed down to his sheaf of grain and their stars all bowed down to his star.

Genesis 37:8 says, "His brothers said to him, 'Do you intend to reign over us? Will you actually rule us?' And they hated him all the more because of his dream and what he had said."

Joseph's father didn't understand the depth of the brothers' hatred or their potential for violence, and he made a tragic error in judgment. Jacob sent Joseph out to check on his brothers while they were tending sheep. Jacob shouldn't have played favorites, shouldn't have tolerated his sons' jealousy of their younger brother, and definitely shouldn't have sent Joseph out alone to meet his angry brothers.

Joseph's brothers exploited and abused him. You're probably familiar with the story: They saw him coming and said, "This is our opportunity. Let's get rid of him!" They attacked him, ripped off the coat his father had given him, beat him, and threw him into a dry cistern, intending to let him die there. When some Ishmaelite traders came by, they sold their own brother into slavery. Joseph, at the age of seventeen, was taken away from everything that was familiar to him—an environment where he was highly favored—and made a lowly slave.

When Your Family Lets You Down

Maybe you grew up in a dysfunctional home or were let down by family members. Maybe your parents were overindulgent, overly permissive, or overly strict, and you still have some scars. Maybe your relatives abused you physically, emotionally, or even sexually, and you still wrestle with the memories, flashbacks, and resentment you have because of those horrible experiences. Perhaps a mate or former spouse let you down by violating the wedding vows or lying to you. Maybe your children have disappointed you. As difficult as those circumstances are to overcome, you don't have to quit or camp—you can keep climbing. Regardless of your past, you can have a high AQ.

I once heard about twin girls who had grown up and were

entirely different. One was an alcoholic and the other totally abstained from alcohol. When the first girl was asked why she had become an alcoholic, she responded, "My dad was an alcoholic. What would you expect me to be?" When the second was asked why she had chosen to abstain from alcohol, she said, "My dad was an alcoholic and I witnessed how it destroyed my family. Wouldn't you expect me to be a total abstainer?" It wasn't genetics or upbringing that determined the girls' future—it was attitude.

Joseph was faithful to God in spite of the fact that his family let him down. When Joseph arrived in Egypt, he became the slave of a man named Potiphar, who was the head of security for Pharaoh. Joseph didn't sulk, refuse to work, or wallow in resentment. He worked hard, determining that if he was to be a slave, he was going to be the best slave he could be.

Joseph's Employer Let Him Down

> Now Joseph had been taken down to Egypt. Potiphar, an Egyptian who was one of Pharaoh's officials, the captain of the guard, bought him from the Ishmaelites who had taken him there. The LORD was with Joseph and he prospered, and he lived in the house of his Egyptian master. When his master saw that the LORD was with him and that the LORD gave him success in everything he did, Joseph found favor in his eyes and became his attendant. Potiphar put him in charge of his household, and he entrusted to his care everything he owned. From the time he put him in charge of his household and of all that he owned, the LORD blessed the household of the Egyptian because of Joseph. The blessing of the LORD was on everything Potiphar had, both in the house and in the field (Genesis 39:1-5).

Life was getting better for Joseph. God was with him. He worked hard, he prospered, and he was promoted. He was put in charge of Potiphar's household. He had been promoted from slave to the chief administrator of Potiphar's estate. Then one day, a different kind of adversity struck Joseph.

> So he left in Joseph's care everything he had; with Joseph in charge, he did not concern himself with anything except the food he ate. Now Joseph was well-built and handsome, and after a while his master's wife took notice of Joseph and said, "Come to bed with me!" (Genesis 39:6, 7).

It's almost never a good idea for two unrelated people of the opposite sex to be alone for prolonged periods of time. No matter how much you trust the other person, no matter the age difference or the social differences, there is too much temptation. As a slave, Joseph was unable to completely avoid the presence of his master's wife, yet he resisted the temptation.

> But he refused. "With me in charge," he told her, "my master does not concern himself with anything in the house; everything he owns he has entrusted to my care. No one is greater in this house than I am. My master has withheld nothing from me except you, because you are his wife. How then could I do such a wicked thing and sin against God?" (Genesis 39:8, 9).

Think about what Joseph could have said had he been trained in the victim mentality of our era: "My brothers hated me, my father was overindulgent with me, my mother died when I was young. I have never known a woman's love. Now here I am, in a foreign country, all alone. My self-esteem has been shattered ever since I became a slave. Everyone in this culture does it anyway, so what does it matter? It's the only way to advance my career and stay out of trouble." Instead, he told himself and his temptress the truth: What she wanted him to do was a wicked thing and a sin against God. Joseph was faithful in spite of continued pressure from Potiphar's wife, and he did his best to avoid the situation. Unfortunately, Potiphar's wife was tenacious too.

> And though she spoke to Joseph day after day, he refused to go to bed with her or even be with her. One day he went into the house to attend to his duties, and none of the household servants was inside. She caught him by his cloak and said, "Come to bed with me!" But he left his cloak in her hand and ran out of the house (Genesis 39:10-12).

It has been said, "Hell hath no fury like a woman scorned." Potiphar's wife would make Joseph pay for wounding her pride.

> She kept his cloak beside her until his master came home. Then she told him this story: "That Hebrew slave you brought us came to me to make sport of me. But as soon as I screamed for help, he left his cloak beside me and ran out of the house." When his master heard the story his wife told him, saying, "This is how your slave treated me," he burned with anger. Joseph's master took him and put him in prison, the place where the king's prisoners were confined (Genesis 39:16-20).

Potiphar sided with his wife and imprisoned Joseph. Joseph had been totally loyal to Potiphar—he did his books, took care of his household, and worked hard. He even refused to respond to the advances of Potiphar's wife, doing exactly what a loyal servant would do. As a result, he was thrown into a miserable prison. Now he was worse than a slave—he was a jailbird. However, Joseph remained faithful to God in spite of this unfair treatment by his employer.

Maybe you've been let down at work. Maybe you gave your lifeblood to a company, then one day your boss came in and said, "We appreciate you but the company's been sold. You no longer have a position." Maybe your boss asked you to do something immoral or dishonest and then demoted you when you didn't respond to his request. Perhaps you worked hard for years and then a relative of the owner was promoted ahead of you, or a coworker undermined you. Maybe you went into a business partnership and your partner exploited you, took advantage of you, falsely accused you, and manipulated money out of you.

When those things happen, you can choose to be devastated, bitter, angry, or resentful, or you can have a high AQ. You can quit, you can camp, or you can climb.

Joseph's Friend Let Him Down

Even in prison, Joseph prospered. A lesser man would have quit. He would have tied his neck to a rope and jumped off a chair in the cell just to get it over with. Even a good guy would have camped out. He would have tolerated it, put in his time, and hoped for something good to happen. But Joseph had an unbelievably high adversity quotient, and he did his best even in prison.

> But while Joseph was there in the prison, the LORD was with him; he showed him kindness and granted him favor in the eyes of the prison warden. So the warden put Joseph in charge of all those held in the prison, and he was made responsible for all that was done there. The warden paid no attention to anything under Joseph's care, because the LORD was with Joseph and gave him success in whatever he did (Genesis 39:20-23).

There were two factors that made Joseph a climber: First, God was with him. God blessed him and showed Joseph favor. Second, Joseph refused to give up. There was a reason that God blessed Joseph—he kept believing, kept persevering, kept giving God opportunities to use him.

One of my favorite stories is about the farmer who showed the new preacher around his farm. The preacher kept saying, "Well, the Lord has a good stand of corn there. The Lord has a beautiful orchard there. The Lord has a nice lake there." The farmer finally got irritated and said, "Preacher, you should have seen this place when the Lord had it all to himself!"

God blesses effort. He asks us to walk the extra mile, work with all our might, make every effort, and not grow weary in doing well. The Bible says, "The sluggard craves and gets nothing, but the desires of the diligent are fully satisfied" (Proverbs 13:4).

But while Joseph was in prison, a friend let him down. Joseph befriended Pharaoh's cupbearer, who had also been thrown into prison. For some reason, Pharaoh had gotten angry at his chief wine taster (the cupbearer) and chief cook (the baker) and threw them both into prison. Pharaoh might have come down with a stomach illness that he suspected was food poisoning, and he knew one of the two men was to blame. Joseph immediately became acquainted with the two men because they were in the cell block that Joseph was overseeing.

One morning, Joseph noticed that both men were dejected and asked them what was wrong. The wine taster said, "We both had vivid, strange dreams last night. They were so distinct and intense that we know they have some meaning, but we haven't a clue what the meaning is. We wish someone could psychoanalyze them for us and interpret the dreams."

"Interpreting dreams is God's business," Joseph said. "Tell me what you saw."

> So the chief cupbearer told Joseph his dream. He said to him, "In my dream I saw a vine in front of me, and on the vine were three branches. As soon as it budded, it blossomed, and its clusters ripened into grapes. Pharaoh's cup was in my hand, and I took the grapes, squeezed them into Pharaoh's cup and put the cup in his hand" (Genesis 40:9-11).

Joseph said, "That's easy. Within three days, Pharaoh will restore you to your position. You're out of here! You're back in the palace. But listen, when you get back to Pharaoh, remember me and get me out of this prison."

The baker was encouraged by Joseph's interpretation and decided to tell Joseph his dream: "I too had a dream: On my head were three baskets of bread. In the top basket were all kinds of baked goods for Pharaoh, but the birds were eating them out of the basket on my head" (Genesis 40:16, 17).

Joseph said, "Mr. Baker, is your insurance paid up? Get your house in order. In three days, Pharaoh will hang you on a tree and birds will eat your flesh." It happened exactly as Joseph had predicted. The baker was found guilty and hanged; the chief cupbearer was restored to his position.

Unfortunately, Joseph's friend the cupbearer let him down. Joseph's kindness was reciprocated by forgetfulness. For two full years, the cupbearer completely forgot about Joseph.

Even friends who have every intention of helping you will let you down because they are people. It may be something minor like forgetting to return a phone call or failing to remember your birthday, or something major like betraying you or stealing your money or your mate. (That reminds me of the old country song, "My wife ran off with my best friend, and boy do I miss him!")

Friends can let you down. Even Jesus was betrayed by a friend. When Judas came out to the Garden of Gethsemane, Jesus said, "Friend, do what you came for" (Matthew 26:50). Judas kissed Him and the soldiers arrested Him.

Years ago, when Dan Issel was playing basketball for the Kentucky Colonels in the old ABA, he invited Judy and me to accompany his wife, Cheri, to watch him play in the all-star game. It was a big event being held in Louisville's Freedom Hall and Dan was going to be the starting forward.

I had already made another commitment that night, so I couldn't go. I was taking eight high school boys to a Cincinnati

Bible College basketball game. I wanted to say to the boys, "I can't go to Cincinnati because I'm going with Dan Issel to the ABA all-star game." I didn't want them to think I was pushing them aside for my own interests, so I kept my commitment.

Four of the boys rode with me. A high school senior, who was also a friend of my family, drove the rest of the team. As we headed home after the game, our cars got separated just outside of Cincinnati on Interstate 75. I got home at 11:30 P.M. About 1:00 A.M., the parents of one of the boys in the other car called and said, "Where's our son? He's not home yet."

I panicked and paced the floor for the next several minutes wondering what to do. I was sure they had been in an accident. Finally, at about 2:00 A.M., I discovered that my friend had deliberately separated from us and driven to a northern Kentucky horse park where there was night racing. The parents were angry with me and with the church, blaming me for being an irresponsible chaperone. The next day, I learned that Dan Issel had been the leading scorer and was voted the most valuable player. I had made this huge sacrifice for those boys and they had kicked me in the teeth. That's when I hired a youth minister!

When a friend betrays you, it's devastating. You believed in him, you were loyal to him, you were convinced he loved you and wanted to be loyal to you. When a friend lets you down, your confidence is shaken and you are tempted to quit on everybody, to just camp out and protect yourself. Joseph was faithful to God in spite of the neglect of his friends. For two years he endured his prison sentence.

The next chapter of Genesis begins by saying, "When two full years had passed, Pharaoh had a dream" (Genesis 41:1). When Pharaoh was looking for someone to interpret his strange dream, the chief cupbearer finally remembered Joseph. He told Pharaoh, "Two years ago I had a dream in prison and there was this guy named Joseph who interpreted it exactly!"

Joseph was summoned out of prison to interpret Pharaoh's

dream. The king was so impressed with Joseph that he appointed him to become the number two man in the land. Guess who now had Joseph as a boss? The cupbearer! Joseph could have called for him and said, "You let me languish in prison for two years. What kind of friend are you?" But there's no indication that Joseph held a grudge. After all he had been through, he probably wasn't surprised that his friend had let him down.

The Lessons We Learn

There are three lessons we learn from Joseph's story that should help us keep climbing when people let us down.

All people are imperfect—expect some disappointment

People aren't 100 percent good or bad. Some are 98 percent good, others are 98 percent bad, and most are somewhere in between. Even the worst people in the world have good qualities. Saddam Hussein probably loves his grandchildren. And even the best people are capable of sin. No one is worthy of our total trust.

Billy Graham made a disappointing statement a few years ago on a television talk show. It contradicted other things he had said about salvation throughout his ministry. He later issued a clarification, but I was reminded that even a man of character like Billy Graham is capable of disappointing you.

Have a high adversity quotient in your relationships

Keep forgiving people, trusting people, and serving people even when they let you down. Don't shrivel up and quit. Don't refuse to trust anyone anymore. Don't become a skeptical, bitter, accusing person.

Joseph never let his disappointments in people destroy him. When his brothers came to Egypt seeking food, he was the one in charge. They bowed down to him just as he had predicted. This was Joseph's chance for revenge, but he didn't retaliate. Instead, he forgave them and provided for their needs. He said, "Don't be distressed and angry with yourselves for what you did to me. God brought me here to save lives. You meant it for evil, but God meant it for good!"

I love the Ten Commandments of Leadership that an anonymous author penned some years ago:

1. People are illogical, unreasonable, and self-centered. Love and trust them anyway.
2. If you do good, people will accuse you of selfish ulterior motives. Do good anyway.
3. If you are successful, you will win false friends and true enemies. Succeed anyway.
4. The service you render today will be forgotten tomorrow. Serve people anyway.
5. Honesty and frankness will make you vulnerable. Be honest and frank anyway.
6. The biggest men with the biggest ideas can be shot down by the smallest men with the smallest ideas. Think big anyway.
7. People pretend to love the "little" people, but sell their souls to the "big" people. Fight for the "little" people anyway.
8. What you spend years building may be destroyed overnight. Build anyway.
9. People really need help, but may attack you if you do help. Help people anyway.
10. Give the world the best you have and you'll get kicked in the teeth. Give the world the best you have anyway.

Put your total trust in Jesus Christ

Jesus is the only one worthy of your complete trust. I don't remember most sermons—even my own!—but there was one sermon I heard thirty-six years ago that I can still remember. To this day I can tell you the outline. Orrin Root, a wonderful man who is still alive and ministering at the age of ninety-six, preached the sermon at my college baccalaureate service in 1965. Here were the three points of his sermon:

- Trust yourself, but not too much.
- Trust other people, but not too much.
- Trust God—and Him you can trust all the way.

My father is one of my heroes because he overcame adversity. He was the seventeenth of eighteen children and his mother died when he was three years old. His father was a heavy drinker and my dad was raised by his older sisters. He had to quit school when he was sixteen to help support the family during the depression, but he managed to return to school two years later and get his high school diploma.

My father married and became a Christian. He worked hard at a job he didn't like for thirty-five years, going every day whether he felt like it or not. (He used a total of five sick days in thirty-five years.) He helped start a new church where he eventually became an elder and the chairman of the board.

My father had six children: two sons who became preachers, two daughters who married preachers, one daughter who remained single and is a Bible teacher and lecturer, and only one daughter who is a black sheep—she married an elder! My father's upbringing left a permanent impression on him. I could see that it impacted his confidence and he was too cautious at times. He wasn't sympathetic with a person who drank. But he became a tough, tenacious human being. His childhood experiences and tremendous faith in God gave him a high AQ. He never quit, and he wasn't hard or bitter. Instead of being a victim, he became a victor. Jesus Christ was the greatest factor in his life, the one who empowered, motivated, and directed my dad's life.

My father believed that you did what you were supposed to do whether you felt like it or not. We went to church every Sunday morning, Sunday night, and Wednesday night regardless of the circumstances.

One Sunday morning, we awakened to discover that sixteen inches of snow had fallen during the night. We thought it was one morning we wouldn't have to go to church. The church was fifteen miles away, but my dad and mom packed all six kids in the car and headed out. A half mile down the road, the car got stuck, and we traipsed back through the snow to our house. My brother and I thought we'd play basketball out in the barn when we got back home. Not so. My dad sat us down in the living room and got out a Bible. He read some Scriptures to us and made some comments. My sister plunked out chords on the piano and we sang hymns together. My mother got out the grape juice and crackers, and we had communion together. I've been a part of remarkable worship services in my lifetime, but that service is still the most memorable one for me.

People sometimes ask me, "Why have you stayed in one church for thirty-five years? Weren't there problems you wanted to escape? Weren't there opportunities in other places that excited you?" I've stayed in Louisville for thirty-five years for the same reason my brother John has preached in one church in northern Kentucky for more than thirty years. By his example, my dad taught us that you don't quit when the snow gets up to your knees. You have a high AQ and keep plowing on.

3

MOSES:
When Feelings of Inferiority
Are Paralyzing,

Faith Acts

Hebrews 11:23-28; Exodus 2:1–4:20

I once heard Harrison Ford, one of Hollywood's leading men, tell an interviewer, "I look at myself on screen and think I look dorky." Actress Bette Davis, considered one of Hollywood's most beautiful women when she was in her prime, said she always felt homely. It's surprising how many people give the impression they're very confident while inside they're struggling with fear.

Even preachers struggle with feelings of inferiority. For several years, I taught a practical ministry class at Kentucky Christian College in the Master of Ministry program. Each minister was required to bring a sermon tape and about ten minutes of the tape would be played in class and critiqued. The men were good preachers with lots of experience, yet it was amazing to observe how embarrassed most of them were to be critiqued by their peers. They almost always made apologies before the critique even began.

Moses Felt Inferior

Moses knew what it meant to feel inferior. Earlier in his life, Moses had tried to act out of support for the Hebrew slaves, but when he murdered one of their Egyptian masters, his fellow Hebrews didn't support him. He fled the country in fear. For forty years, he quietly herded sheep in Midian, minded his own business, raised a family, and tried to forget about his people still suffering in Egypt. That's when God called to him from a burning bush, instructing Moses to go to Pharaoh and demand the release of the Hebrew slaves. God had been preparing Moses all of his life for this one assignment.

It was an intimidating assignment. Pharaoh was the most powerful, ruthless leader in the world. Who would dare to confront Pharaoh? There were almost two million uneducated Hebrew slaves in Egypt. How could Moses persuade them to follow him out of Egypt? Could he sneak two million people over the border? Could the Egyptians be persuaded to give up their slaves? Anyone demanding the abolition of slavery in Egypt would be the laughingstock of the country and would jeopardize his life. So even though God was talking to him from a burning bush, Moses was so intimidated by the assignment that he dared to question God.

> But Moses said to God, "Who am I, that I should go to
> Pharaoh and bring the Israelites out of Egypt?" And God
> said, "I will be with you. And this will be the sign to you that
> it is I who have sent you: When you have brought the people
> out of Egypt, you will worship God on this mountain"
> (Exodus 3:11, 12).

Mount Horeb, where God appeared in the burning bush, was also called Mount Sinai—the place where God gave Moses the Ten Commandments. God kept His word. God always does what He says He will do.

Moses submitted one objection after another as he spoke to God at the burning bush: "Who shall I say sent me?" God said, "Tell them the I Am sent you." "What if they don't believe me and scoff at me?" God said, "I'll give you miraculous power so that you will gain credibility." "But I'm not a good speaker!" God said,

"I made your tongue. I'll help you, and I'll send your brother Aaron to help you." Finally, Moses just pleaded, "Lord, I don't want to go. Please send someone else."

The Problem of Inferiority

In his book, *What Wives Wish Their Husbands Knew About Women*, Dr. James Dobson suggests that the major cause of depression among women is low self-esteem. He describes the troubling thoughts flowing through the mind of someone struggling with inferiority:

> It is sitting alone in a house during the quiet afternoon hours, wondering why the phone doesn't ring . . . wondering why you have no "real" friends. It is longing for someone to talk to, soul-to-soul, but knowing there is no such person worthy of your trust. It is feeling that "they wouldn't like me if they knew the real me." It is becoming terrified when speaking to a group of your peers, and feeling like a fool when you get home. It is wondering why other people have so much more talent and ability than you do. It is feeling incredibly ugly and sexually unattractive. It is admitting that you have become a failure as a wife and mother. It is disliking everything about yourself and wishing, constantly wishing, you could be someone else. It is feeling unloved and unlovable and lonely and sad. It is lying in bed after the family is asleep, pondering the vast emptiness inside and longing for unconditional love. It is intense self-pity. It is reaching up in the darkness to remove a tear from the corner of your eye. It is depression![8]

Such feelings of inferiority can cause paralyzing fear that hinders us from following God's call. And it's not just women. It's men and children too. Even godly people like Moses. In fact, most of us can identify with Moses' feelings of inferiority—but not everyone does. You may be one of those rare people who feels very confident in yourself. Maybe all of your life you've been able to achieve—you were the star athlete, top student, homecoming queen, class president. Now you're a business whiz and successful by the world's standards, and you can't understand why other people have inhibitions or feelings of inadequacy. When we sing "How Great Thou Art," you're tempted to stand up and wave as if it's a personal tribute! But most of us know what it is like to struggle with a sense of inadequacy.

Why are so many plagued with feelings of inferiority?

Negative programming from childhood

Sometimes the problem is the negative programming people received in their childhood. If your parents or other significant people in your life left the impression that you were unwanted or unworthy, or that no matter what you did it was never good enough, it can create feelings of inferiority. If you constantly heard things like, "You'll never amount to anything," or "If there's a wrong way to do it, you'll find it," then it's no surprise that you battle an inferiority complex. You were always trying to earn approval rather than being the recipient of unconditional love.

Moses was the product of two different homes. His mother reared him until he was old enough to live in the palace, when Pharaoh's daughter adopted him. No doubt this Jewish boy growing up in an Egyptian environment battled rumors about his heritage, rivalry with his siblings, name-calling, and feelings of being an outcast.

Cultural expectations

Our society places a high premium on appearance, possessions, athletic prowess, and youth. If you aren't built like Arnold Schwarzenegger or your thighs aren't as thin as Cindy Crawford's, you feel inadequate. If you can't dunk a basketball or afford the nicest clothes, you feel inferior to others around you. Christian apologist Josh McDowell once said,

The health of an entire society depends on the ease with which the individual members gain personal acceptance. Thus, whenever the keys to self-esteem are seemingly out of reach for a large percentage of the people, as in twentieth-century America, then widespread mental illness, neuroticism, hatred, alcoholism, drug abuse, violence and social disorder will occur.[9]

Moses had worked as a lowly shepherd for forty years. That was one of the most despised occupations in Egypt. Maybe he felt inferior because of cultural comparisons.

Past failure

Moses would never forget the rejection he felt when the Hebrew slaves didn't respond to his leadership. Now God was asking him to go back into the same arena where he'd already been knocked down, and try to lead those same people.

If you tried to make the team and got cut, if you started your own business and lost money, if you were jilted by someone you loved, your confidence is severely shaken, especially in that particular area. No matter how many things you have accomplished, a failure wounds you. The injury stays in your mind long after recovery is complete.

Satanic influence

The primary source of inferiority is Satan. The Bible commands us to love our neighbors as ourselves (Matthew 19:19). Husbands are told to love their wives as their own bodies (Ephesians 5:28). It is not God's will for us to be self-loathing and self-deprecating. Satan wants us to be intimidated and to despise ourselves because inferiority negates our effectiveness. Jesus described Satan as a thief and liar. Satan lies about your value and robs you of your sense of worth.

Dr. David Seamands writes in his book, *Healing for Damaged Emotions:*

Satan's greatest psychological weapon is a gut-level feeling of inferiority, inadequacy and low self-worth. This feeling shackles many Christians in spite of their faith and knowledge of God's Word. Although they understand their position as sons and daughters of God, they are tied up in knots, bound by a terrible feeling of inferiority and chained to a deep sense of worthlessness.[10]

The Consequences of Inferiority

In that same book, Dr. Seamands mentions four negative consequences of inferiority.[11]

Inferiority paralyzes your potential

Moses said, "God, I'm not a good speaker." That probably wasn't altogether true. Josephus, a Jewish historian, wrote that Moses had been a general in Pharaoh's army during his earlier years, so Moses had experience leading people and speaking in front of many men. Stephen related in Acts 7 that Moses was "powerful in speech and action." Moses had the necessary ability to be God's spokesman, but insecurity had paralyzed him.

You may be gifted to lead, teach, write, minister, discover, design, or build. God may want you to create jobs, lift spirits, educate minds, heal hurts, or save souls. But if you keep backing away from challenges because you don't believe you can do them, you don't lack confidence in yourself—you lack confidence in God.

Remember the one-talent man in Jesus' parable (Matthew 25)? Rather than invest the money his master had entrusted to him, he buried it in the ground. He explained to his master that he was *afraid*. He felt inferior to the two-talent man and the five-talent man, so he did nothing. His potential was frozen by his fear of rejection.

Satan wants you to feel so inferior that you settle down in a job and live far below your potential. Christ wants you to develop your gifts to the fullest so that you can be a positive influence for Him and live life abundantly. He wants you to say with Paul, "I can do everything through him who gives me strength" (Philippians 4:13).

Inferiority destroys your dreams

Forty years earlier, Moses couldn't tolerate watching the abuse of a fellow Hebrew. He passionately envisioned his people being freed. He took the wrong course of action—instead of waiting for God's timing, he took matters into his own hands and murdered a taskmaster—but it was the right dream. Then, when God said, "I want you to go to Pharaoh and demand the release of my people," Moses wasn't interested. Inferiority had killed his dream.

Acts 2:17 predicts that one of the signs of the Holy Spirit being poured out is that the "young men will see visions" and the "old men will dream dreams." What has happened to your dreams? Have you lost the idealism of youth?

I don't mean that we should dwell on unrealistic fantasies. Some dreams are far-fetched and impractical. Someone said that *neurotics* can be defined as people who build castles in the air, *psychotics* are those who move into them, and *psychiatrists* are the ones who collect the rent! I'm not asking you to live in a dream world, but to allow God to restore your hope. "Where there is no vision, the people perish" (Proverbs 29:18, *KJV*).

In Numbers 13, 14, we read that after their release from Egypt, God planted another bold dream in the children of Israel. He promised them "a land flowing with milk and honey." God brought them right up to the edge of the land and said, "Now I want you to go in and possess it." Moses sent the best man from each of the twelve tribes to spy out the land. The scouts came back saying, "The land is beautiful! We've never seen grapes and pomegranates so large. The honey is the sweetest we've ever tasted. *But . . .* the cities are well fortified, and the people are like giants. We are like grasshoppers in their sight." You can't have a much lower self-concept than to see yourself as a grasshopper.

As a result of their inferiority complex, the dream was destroyed. The people began weeping and wallowing in self-pity. As a consequence, they were forced to wander in the wilderness for forty years until a new generation—a people full of hope and vision—could be raised up to take the land. God's dream wasn't a neurotic air castle; it was a reality He wanted to give them. It was within their reach. The land was ready, God was ready, the dream was ready, but the people weren't ready because of their low self-esteem and lack of faith in God. They forgot they were children of God.

If Satan has tricked you into thinking of yourself as a grasshopper, you have no room to dream. You're filled with doubts and fear, and you underestimate what God wants to do through you.

When I was a sophomore in Bible college, my roommate looked out the window and saw the sharpest-looking freshman girl walking across campus. She was not only pretty, she was wealthy. She owned a new Chevy Impala convertible, which was rare on campus! As you can imagine, she was the center of all the guys' attention. My roommate said, "Wow, I'm going to ask her out." I thought, *Who do you think you are? You are going to get shot down.* About a year later, they got married! I thought, *There's a lesson here.* Where there is no vision, the people perish. If you don't dream, you can't achieve, and God can't achieve great things through you.

Inferiority ruins relationships

Inferiority not only paralyzes your potential and destroys your dreams, it also ruins your relationships.

It ruins your relationship with God. If you think of yourself as worthless, how does that reflect on the one who created you? If you're convinced the design is wrong, it's not long before you become resentful of the Designer. You will begin to question, "Lord, why didn't you create *me* with a more attractive body? Why am *I* not more talented? Why couldn't *I* have been that smart?" A poor self-concept ruins your relationship with God. You'll eventually conclude that He doesn't care much for you. If you can't love yourself, it will be difficult to love the one who created you.

It ruins your relationships with others. David Seamands wrote,

> Satan uses your nagging sense of inferiority and inadequacy to isolate you. . . . The most common way to cope with feelings of inferiority is to pull within yourself, to have as little contact with other people as you possibly can, and just occasionally peek out as the rest of the world goes by.[12]

The most difficult people to get along with are those who don't like themselves. If you feel inferior, then you get your feelings hurt easily, you're overly suspicious and defensive, and you probably withdraw from people when your ego gets wounded. If you are plagued by feelings of inadequacy, you are constantly asking—either directly or indirectly—for others to make you feel competent. You're a praise-a-holic, always needing an ego boost. You may not even realize how much of a drain your demands put on your family and friends. When you're so absorbed in your own need for encouragement, you don't have anything left to give to others.

Moses was perfectly content to isolate himself out in the desert. He wanted nothing to do with the Hebrew slaves. His confidence had been shattered once, when he had tried to help and the people rejected him. Why subject himself to the possibility of that happening again?

Inferiority sabotages Christian service

God selected Moses to lead, but Moses said, "Send somebody else. I'm not qualified." God has equipped everyone in the body of Christ with distinctive gifts so the body can function properly. Unfortunately, the first thing many of us say when we're asked to participate is, "I'm not capable." Or, "I couldn't serve as a leader. There are so many more capable people. I'd be intimidated." Or,

"I couldn't participate in a drama or sing in the choir. I'd be a nervous wreck!" Or, "Don't ask me to give a testimony in front of those people. I'll get tongue-tied." Or, "I couldn't visit in the hospital. I don't know those people, and I'm not much of a people-person." Or, "I couldn't lead a support group. I've got my own problems."

A lack of self-confidence imprisons you in fear and negates your service. God doesn't choose superstars to do His work—He chooses servants. Maybe Moses really did have a speech problem. Maybe he stuttered. We know he was a lowly shepherd, he was getting older, and he had failed in his past. Yet God takes people with shortcomings and gives them the grace they need to perform the task He's asking them to do. "Brothers, think of what you were when you were called. Not many of you were wise by human standards; not many were influential; not many were of noble birth" (1 Corinthians 1:26). There aren't many supermen or wonderwomen on God's team.

Years ago, a local newscaster in our town told me that the first Sunday he came to church, he looked at the two men sitting on the platform—the song leader and me—and made some observations. He said, "No offense, Bob, but the song leader was much more impressive-looking than you were. He was bigger, more handsome, and a little younger. I thought to myself, *I hope the one on the left is the speaker.*" How disappointed he was when the speaker turned out to be me!

A woman from Shelbyville, Kentucky, came up to me after church one day and said, "I've listened to you on the radio for years and I came today to see what you looked like."

"Well," I snickered, "What do you think?"

"I had to keep my head down the whole time. I just couldn't believe that voice was coming out of that body!" she said.

God often uses very ordinary people so that *He* gets the glory and not man. When inferiority and fear paralyze us, we rob God of a marvelous opportunity to show His power and ability through our infirmities. Paul wrote, "But [God] said to me, 'My grace is sufficient for you, for my power is made perfect in weakness.' Therefore I will boast all the more gladly about my weaknesses, so that Christ's power may rest on me" (2 Corinthians 12:9).

The Cure for Inferiority

If you're hoping I will give you some magic formula that you can take for an overnight cure, you'll be disappointed. The title of a popular book says, *Be Your Own Best Friend*, as if all of your problems would be solved if you'd love yourself more than anything else. That's not the solution for curing an inferiority complex. In fact, pride is one of the *problems*, and if you allow your ego to get out of control, you will exacerbate the situation. There are two important attitude choices that must take place in your life in order for you to overcome feelings of inferiority and increase your faith.

Surrender to God

God didn't cure Moses' inferiority complex by saying, "Moses, let's talk about your upbringing in the palace. Let's get in touch with your inner potential." God's anger was kindled against Moses and He said, "You go and do what I command." Moses finally swallowed his pride and surrendered to God's authority in his life. He decided to take a step of faith and obey.

The first step to overcoming inferiority is to acknowledge that God is in charge of your life and you are not. A servant isn't concerned with promoting or fulfilling himself. He's concerned with obedience and seeks to fulfill the desires of the master. If he feels inadequate, he does them anyway. If he feels afraid, he obeys anyway. If he thinks it might be embarrassing, he does what he's told anyway. When you begin to trust God and acknowledge His sovereignty over you, then you become concerned with exalting Him and not yourself. That's when you begin to feel valuable.

The philosophy of this world tells you to believe in your *inherent* value. "You have self-worth," the world says. "You have unlimited potential. Stand up for your rights. Practice self-actualization!" However, the absolute truth is that you don't have any value apart from God. There are six billion people in the world. About 5.999999 billion don't know who you are and don't care. You might get a little notoriety in this world, but one day you are going to die and most people won't miss you.

I'll tell you something humbling but true: The attendance at your funeral will be affected by whether it rains that day. And though most of the people who do come will cry during your funeral, they'll be back home laughing and eating potato salad within an hour. The Bible says, "What is your life? You are a mist that appears for a little while and then vanishes" (James 4:14).

The good news is that when you surrender to the sovereignty of God and begin to have faith in God's ability to use you, then you become valuable. Ian Pitman Watson said, "There are some things that are loved because they are valuable; there are other things that are valuable because they are loved."

When my son Rusty was two years old, he went to the hospital to have eye surgery. Someone gave him a stuffed brown dog with long floppy ears. It had a huge red bow around its neck. He loved that dog and took it to bed every night. It curled perfectly under his arm where it remained all night long, every night. When he was four years old, he had eye surgery again, and the dog went with him to the hospital. *I* carried it for him! Even after he had outgrown taking it to bed with him, that dog remained a part of the decor of his room for years. His mother still keeps it in a special box as a memento of the past. It has lost all its fuzziness, the red bow is long gone, its tongue has fallen out, one eye is missing, and it is little more than a rag, but it has never been thrown away. Some things are loved because they're valuable, but other things are valuable because they're loved.

When you surrender to the sovereignty of God, He adopts you

into His family and you become a child of the King of kings. He loves you so much that He came to this earth to die for you. You are of value, not because of what you are, but because of *whose* you are.

Serve others

The second step to overcoming inferiority is to forget yourself and focus on the challenge of helping others. The world will tell you just the opposite: "Look out for number one. The first thing you have to do is love yourself. Look inward and understand what makes you tick." Moses was looking out for number one, and God in essence said to him, "Look, Moses. There are two million people in slavery who need to be freed. Quit thinking about whether you're a good speaker or whether you'll be embarrassed, and start thinking about them. Go do what I said to do."

You may be so self-conscious that you live by fear, always trying to avoid making mistakes that could embarrass you. Jesus said, "For whoever wants to save his life will lose it, but whoever loses his life for me will find it" (Matthew 16:25). Jesus' advice is to forget about yourself and focus on others, for the sake of Christ.

Popular motivational speaker Cavitt Robert says, "If you worry too much about what people think of you, you'll probably be disappointed to discover how seldom they do!" When you get your mind off of yourself and start focusing on serving others, two things happen:

People's needs are met. Others will be helped by your uninhibited use of your gifts. Respected Christian author Elmer Towns tells a story about a motorcycle gang member who became convicted that he needed to begin going to church. This big, bearded, longhaired man walked into a small church building one Sunday morning and strode right up to the front row as the congregation stared. His heart was softened by the message that day and he knew God was working on him. At the end of the service, the preacher announced that there was an extreme need for volunteers in the nursery and asked if anyone would be willing to volunteer for next week. There was no response, so the preacher reiterated the need and asked again. The biker prayed silently, "Lord, let me know what to do. If you want me to volunteer, have him ask a third time."

The preacher said, "Without a volunteer, we will not be able to provide a nursery next week," and he made a *third* appeal: "Would someone please volunteer next week in the nursery?" The biker looked around and slowly began to raise his hand. Immediately fifty women jumped to their feet to volunteer. Problem solved![13]

When you use your gifts, other people are inspired to serve. When you quit worrying about what people will think of you and start considering how you can help meet needs, God will begin using you in dramatic ways.

Your feelings of self-worth are enhanced. When you serve others, you also feel better about yourself. Someone asked the noted psychologist Dr. Karl Menninger what to do when you feel the onslaught of a nervous breakdown. You might have expected Dr. Menninger to prescribe a vacation—take some time off to get away from your problems. But he responded, "I think if I felt insecure, I would go out the door, go across the tracks, find someone in need, and do something to help them." Mental health is contingent upon ministering to others. Jesus said, "The greatest among you will be your servant" (Matthew 23:11).

When I was a teenager, I read an article that I've never forgotten. It was about two friends who were competing in a state diving competition. The main character, Jimmy, was a mediocre diver, but his friend Billy had the potential to be the state champion. Yet whenever they got into competition, Billy always froze. He didn't do nearly as well under pressure. When the two practiced together, Jimmy always thought, *If Billy could dive in competition the way he does in practice, he'd win every time.*

At the state meet, Jimmy got an idea. He would talk to Billy throughout the competition as he did when they were practicing.

So when he stepped to the diving board, he yelled, "Watch this Billy, I'm an eagle. See if you can top this!" or, "O.K., Billy. I'm going to reach the rafters with this one!" or, "Billy, I'm a swan!" Jimmy's plan worked. Billy seemed to relax, and he did as well as he did in practice. Billy was outstanding.

When the awards were announced, Billy didn't receive first place. He was given the second-place medal. Who was the state champion? It was Jimmy! Jimmy had become so engrossed in helping his friend that he had reached a higher potential than he had ever dreamed possible. "The greatest among you will be the servant of all."

Through faith Moses obeyed God and accomplished great things. He went to Egypt as God had commanded, and he demanded the release of the Hebrews.

> By faith he left Egypt, not fearing the king's anger; he perse-
> vered because he saw him who is invisible. By faith he kept
> the Passover and the sprinkling of blood, so that the destroy-
> er of the firstborn would not touch the firstborn of Israel. By
> faith the people passed through the Red Sea as on dry land;
> but when the Egyptians tried to do so, they were drowned
> (Hebrews 11:27-29).

Moses led the people of Israel across the Red Sea and through the wilderness. He received the Ten Commandments from God. He trained the people and prepared them for the promised land. He wrote the first five books of the Old Testament. Yet when you read his story, you often get the feeling that Moses would rather have been somewhere else. He continued to battle an inferiority complex, but he obeyed anyway. He surrendered to the sovereignty of God in his life and had faith that God could use him. Moses sacrificed himself so that his people could be free. "By faith he left Egypt, not fearing the king's anger; he persevered *because he saw him who is invisible*" (Hebrews 11:27).

4

RAHAB:
When Security Is Appealing,
Faith Takes Risks

Hebrews 11:31; Joshua 2:1-21; 6:22-25

More than 150,000 people a year risk their lives "shooting the rapids" down the Colorado River. In the last thirty years, more than 45,000 people have taken up the hobby of hang gliding, strapping gossamer wings on their backs and jumping off cliffs in hopes that the air will catch them and they will gradually float to the earth below.[14] Thousands of people each day enter the stock market for the first time, risking their money in hopes that they can make more. Thousands of people in the last few years have tried bungee jumping—leaping off a sixty-foot crane or bridge with a bungee chord strapped to their backs. Churchill Downs, the home of the Kentucky Derby in Louisville, advertises for new betting customers by urging people to "add a genuine risk to your life."

Some people love taking risks. They like the rush of adrenaline and the feeling of escaping the ordinary. But most of us are not risk takers. Most of us are security seekers, committed to a life of playing it safe. We hedge our bets, cover our tracks, and touch all the bases. From being overinsured to eating low-fat diets, most of us try to minimize risk taking as much as possible. We don't mind the idea of taking risks, as long as it's somebody else doing it. We'll stand in awe of someone willing to walk a tightrope and say, "Look at that crazy guy," but we would rather have a life free of pressure and uncertainty.

Jesus made it clear that following Him would be a risky life of action, adventure, and expansion. "I will follow you wherever you go," one man said. Jesus responded, "The Son of Man has no place to lay his head." In other words, "Are you sure you want to risk your safety and security to follow me?"

Another man offered to follow Jesus if he could first return and say good-bye to everybody. Jesus said, "No one who puts his hand to the plow and looks back is fit for service in the kingdom of God" (Luke 9:58-62). Jesus wants you to risk everything you have to follow Him. He told a rich man to give up all his possessions to follow Him. In the parable of the talents, Jesus chastised the one-talent man for refusing to take a risk with his money.

Jesus commands you to deny yourself, take up your cross, and follow Him. Carrying a cross is risky business! Following Christ is a life of challenge and adventure. It is not a life for the faint of heart.

A Risk Taker

The prostitute Rahab is not someone you'd expect to see in the list of heroes of the faith in Hebrews 11. Yet there she is, right behind Moses, in the same list with Abraham, Isaac, Jacob, and Joseph. "By faith the prostitute Rahab, because she welcomed the spies, was not killed with those who were disobedient" (Hebrews 11:31). Rahab is given more space than Samson, David, and Gideon. Here is a woman who had lived a life of sin, but at just the right moment, she took one risky step of faith that made all the difference in her life. Her one step of faith vaulted her into heroine status.

Moses' successor, Joshua, the leader of the Israelites, was preparing to lead the people of Israel across the Jordan River into the promised land. Joshua sent two men to spy out the city of Jericho—the first city they would face after crossing the river.

> Then Joshua son of Nun secretly sent two spies from Shittim.
> "Go, look over the land," he said, "especially Jericho." So
> they went and entered the house of a prostitute named
> Rahab and stayed there (Joshua 2:1).

After spying out the land around Jericho all day, the two spies
entered Rahab's house to spend the night. They probably suspected that no one would question the motives of two visitors if they
spent the night at a prostitute's house. However, the king of
Jericho somehow discovered their purpose and whereabouts and
sent soldiers to Rahab's house to bring out the spies. Should they
be brought before the king, they would surely be put to death.

> So the king of Jericho sent this message to Rahab: "Bring out
> the men who came to you and entered your house, because
> they have come to spy out the whole land." But the woman
> had taken the two men and hidden them. She said, "Yes, the
> men came to me, but I did not know where they had come
> from. At dusk, when it was time to close the city gate, the
> men left. I don't know which way they went. Go after them
> quickly. You may catch up with them" (Joshua 2:3-5).

Rahab hid the two men on her roof under the stalks of flax.
Then she lied to the soldiers about their whereabouts. "You know,
those two men did come by tonight," she grinned, "but they paid
their bill and left. Sorry, fellas. I didn't know they were spies, so I
didn't watch which way they went. I bet if you boys hurried, you
could still catch those nasty bad guys!"

Rahab is considered a hero because of a lie she told. More than
once in the Old Testament, those who lied to protect the lives of
innocent people were not held accountable for their lying. In
Exodus 1, we read that the Hebrew midwives Shiphrah and Puah
hid the babies from the wicked Pharaoh who wanted to kill them.
When Pharaoh asked them why more babies weren't being killed,

the midwives lied, saying, "The women are giving birth before we can get there!" The Scripture says God blessed the midwives because of their actions and gave them families of their own.

We wouldn't think of casting judgment on a Christian family who hid Jews in their home during the Holocaust, even if they lied to the Nazi authorities in order to save the lives of those innocent people. In the same way, Rahab and the Hebrew midwives are not condemned for lying to save peoples' lives.

More important than what she did in hiding the two spies was why Rahab took this bold risk. When the soldiers were gone, she said to the spies:

> I know that the LORD has given this land to you and that a great fear of you has fallen on us, so that all who live in this country are melting in fear because of you. We have heard how the LORD dried up the water of the Red Sea for you when you came out of Egypt, and what you did to Sihon and Og, the two kings of the Amorites east of the Jordan, whom you completely destroyed. When we heard of it, our hearts melted and everyone's courage failed because of you, for the LORD your God is God in heaven above and on the earth below (Joshua 2:9-11).

This pagan prostitute had discovered who the one true God was, and she knew she didn't want to cross Him. Courage isn't the absence of fear; sometimes courage just means your fear is in the right place! Jesus said, "But I tell you that men will have to give account on the day of judgment for every careless word they have spoken" (Matthew 12:36). Imagine how much sin people could avoid if they were more afraid of facing God on Judgment Day than they were of letting people down, being ridiculed, or missing out on some fun.

Rahab knew she had reason to fear the God who had sent His people to take over the land that was rightfully theirs. She feared

God's impending judgment more than she feared anything else. And she was willing to risk everything she had—her livelihood, her home, even her life—to be on God's side. Rahab said to the two spies:

> Now then, please swear to me by the LORD that you will show kindness to my family, because I have shown kindness to you. Give me a sure sign that you will spare the lives of my father and mother, my brothers and sisters, and all who belong to them, and that you will save us from death (Joshua 2:12, 13).

Risking It All for the Cause of Christ

The things that Rahab risked are the very things many Christians have risked for the cause of Christ and the very things God calls you to risk for His sake today.

Your security

A friend asked the farmer, "How's your corn doing this year?"

He said, "I didn't plant any this year. I thought it might be too dry."

"Oh, then how are your beans?" the friend asked.

The farmer said, "I didn't plant any. I don't think the prices will be worth it."

"O.K. How's your wheat doing?"

"I didn't plant any. I anticipate some spring floods that will wash out the crop."

Finally the friend asked, "What did you plant?"

The farmer responded, "I didn't plant anything this year. I'm just playing it safe."

As bad as Rahab's life as a prostitute must have been, it was her life. It was what she was used to. So often even people in the worst of circumstances, ruined by sinful lifestyles, won't come to God because they are comfortable with the familiar. They're willing to just play it safe.

While the men hid upstairs, Rahab must have thought about her life. Rahab knew that putting her trust in God and the inevitable future that He would bring meant change in her life. She could have told them all was clear and said, "Now get lost. I never want to see you two Israelites again." She could have played it safe and decided to believe that there really wasn't a God of the Israelites and that the city of Jericho would be spared. Instead, she determined to act upon what she knew to be true even though it meant risking her familiar life. She told the two men that she wanted her life—and the lives of her family members—to be spared, even if everything else around her was destroyed and they were forced to live among the Israelites.

You can go a lifetime avoiding risk, avoiding commitments, and making no decision at all about following Christ. You might think you're playing it safe, but you will lose everything. Jesus said, "For whoever wants to save his life will lose it, but whoever loses his life for me and for the gospel will save it" (Mark 8:35).

When I was eleven years old, my Little League baseball team went swimming at a public pool. I remember swimming with all the kids and looking over at my dad sitting in a chair by the edge of the water. I felt a little sorry for him. He was an excellent swimmer, he loved the water, and it was so hot that day. But he hadn't brought his swim trunks, so there he sat with the coaches, just watching us.

A few minutes later, I glanced up and saw my dad jumping in the water with all his clothes on. I thought my dad had gone berserk! It was hot, but that was a little extreme. I thought, "Oh no! The other kids are going to think my dad is so weird!" What I didn't know was that Roger, a young man with the common sense of an eggplant, had jumped off the diving board not realizing the water was over his head, and Roger couldn't swim. I watched my dad race to Roger and pull him to safety. The boys didn't think my dad was a fanatic—he was a hero! The reward of a saved life was well worth the risk of a wet ride home. On the other hand, Roger was a fanatic. The thrill of a jump off the diving board wasn't worth the risk of drowning.

The world may think you're fanatical if you risk everything for Christ because they don't understand the cause. It may make them uneasy because they don't realize what's at stake or understand God's faithfulness.

After Rebecca Gander graduated from Georgetown College, she decided to do a year's internship in Vietnam, a country that is closed to Christianity. Because she couldn't enter as a missionary, she went as a math and English teacher with hopes of having the opportunity to plant seeds of the gospel in the minds of her students. About six months into her service, her father approached me at church one day and said, "I won't be seeing much of Rebecca anymore." I asked why, and he responded, "She loves what she is doing so much that she's decided to stay full time."

Jesus said, "Anyone who loves his father or mother more than me is not worthy of me; anyone who loves his son or daughter more than me is not worthy of me; and anyone who does not take his cross and follow me is not worthy of me" (Matthew 10:37, 38).

Your livelihood

Surely Rahab knew that following the one true God would mean giving up her lifestyle. What would she do for a living if all her clientele were dead and she was forced to live with a bunch of God-fearing people?

For some people, coming to God means risking your career. If you're an abortion doctor, prostitute, or drug dealer, you know that following God means giving up that business. That's obvious, but there are other situations where the lines are a little fuzzier. If you're a cocktail waitress, casino worker, or bartender, you might conclude that even though your job doesn't require you to personally violate any of God's commands, you're encouraging others toward immoral behavior and putting yourself in compromising situations. God might be calling you to give up your profession.

If you're an actor, you may be invited to take part in a movie, show, advertisement, or play that demeans your values and could damage your testimony. You might say, "If I turn this down, my career will be ruined." God calls you to take that risk.

If you're an employee with a corrupt boss, you may have to decide you can't continue to work in an environment where you're supporting illegal or immoral activity. Leaving your profession because you believe God is calling you to do so is risky business, but that's what Rahab did.

That's what Paul did, too. Paul had been a young, ambitious politician. Then he met Jesus Christ and gave it all up to follow Him. He wrote:

> But whatever was to my profit I now consider loss for the sake of Christ. What is more, I consider everything a loss compared to the surpassing greatness of knowing Christ Jesus my Lord, for whose sake I have lost all things. I consider them rubbish, that I may gain Christ and be found in him, not having a righteousness of my own that comes from the law, but that which is through faith in Christ—the righteousness that comes from God and is by faith (Philippians 3:7-9).

Festus, a contemporary of Paul's who was also a politician, heard Paul's story. "You are out of your mind, Paul!" he shouted. "Your great learning is driving you insane."

"I am not insane, most excellent Festus," Paul replied. "What I am saying is true and reasonable" (Acts 26:24, 25). When you understand the true stakes, risking your career to follow Christ is reasonable.

Many Christians today are still giving up their livelihood and possessions for the cause of Christ. Former football coach Bill

McCartney gave up his career to start Promise Keepers. Some, like Jim and Jacque Baumgardner from our church, have even left their careers to enter the mission field. Jim was a social worker and Jacque was a receptionist at our church. They were both comfortable with their jobs and loved our church. Then they went on two short-term mission trips to Bosnia. Visiting that troubled area was risky enough, but after those trips, they felt led to be full-time missionaries in Bosnia. Today they are living in that difficult area, ministering faithfully and rejoicing in each victory God gives them.

Your life

After the soldiers left Rahab's house, she helped the two spies escape. Her house was located on the city wall, so she took a scarlet cord and helped them slip out of the second-floor window and down the outside of the city wall. Once they were safely on the ground, they said to her:

> This oath you made us swear will not be binding on us
> unless, when we enter the land, you have tied this scarlet
> cord in the window through which you let us down, and
> unless you have brought your father and mother, your broth-
> ers and all your family into your house. If anyone goes out-
> side your house into the street, his blood will be on his own
> head; we will not be responsible. As for anyone who is in the
> house with you, his blood will be on our head if a hand is
> laid on him (Joshua 2:17-19).

If Rahab had been discovered hiding the Israelite spies, she surely would have been put to death. Now that the spies were gone, what if someone found out what she had done before the Israelites returned and took over the city? Her life would be over. Or what if she was wrong? What if the Israelites attacked the city and didn't win the battle? Or what if they became afraid, refused to fight against Jericho, and never returned? People would ask a lot of questions about that scarlet cord. Someone would surely conclude what she had done.

Rahab's belief in God was so strong that she feared God's wrath on her city more than she feared all of the other possibilities. She was willing to risk her life and the lives of her family members. It must have seemed strange to the others in the city that Rahab was hanging a scarlet cord from her window and was cramming all of her relatives into her home, but she didn't care what others thought. She was willing to take that small risk to save the lives of those she loved.

When Joshua and the Israelites came to destroy the city of Jericho, we read:

> Joshua said to the two men who had spied out the land, "Go into the prostitute's house and bring her out and all who belong to her, in accordance with your oath to her." So the young men who had done the spying went in and brought out Rahab, her father and mother and brothers and all who belonged to her. They brought out her entire family and put them in a place outside the camp of Israel. Then they burned the whole city and everything in it. . . . But Joshua spared Rahab the prostitute, with her family and all who belonged to her, because she hid the men Joshua had sent as spies to Jericho—and she lives among the Israelites to this day (Joshua 6:22-25).

Throughout much of the history of the church, confessing Christ as Lord has meant risking your life. Many early Christians lost their lives as a result of that risk. Stephen was stoned, James was beheaded, and Peter was crucified upside down. The famous *Foxe's Book of Martyrs* recounts dozens of stories of Christians throughout history who, in the words of Revelation 12:11, "did not love their lives so much as to shrink from death." The world labeled them as fanatical, but God classifies them as faithful. And today in heaven, they know they took the right risk.

Standing for Christ today may mean risking your life. Many in foreign countries are routinely persecuted and even killed for their faith in Christ. Even in America people have been shot in their schools or churches for gathering to pray or saying they believed in God.

The famous missionary Jim Elliot and four of his friends were killed by the Auca Indians they were trying to reach for Christ. The world must have thought, "What a waste. What a tragedy that these five young men were killed." But as the son of one of those five men later wrote:

> God took five common young men of uncommon commitment and used them for his own glory. They never had the privilege they so enthusiastically pursued to tell the Huaorani of the God they loved and served. But . . . there are a thousand [missionaries] who follow God's trail more resolutely because of their example. This success withheld from them in life God multiplied and continues to multiply as a memorial to their obedience and his faithfulness.[15]

Even the very tribe that killed the young missionaries eventually heard the gospel, and many responded when the wives of the missionaries visited years later.[16]

So what about you? Are you willing to risk losing your security to do what you believe God wants you to do? Are you willing to risk all that you have—your career, your ambitions, even your life—for the cause of Christ? Jesus promised, "Everyone who has left houses or brothers or sisters or father or mother or children or fields for my sake will receive a hundred times as much and will inherit eternal life" (Matthew 19:29).

Risking those things may seem fanatical to some, but only because they haven't put their faith in the one who created them— the one who risked all He had to come to this earth to die for them and promised to reward them a hundred times over for those things they have risked. Jim Elliot had written in his diary, "He is no fool who exchanges that which he cannot keep for that which he can never lose."

5

JOSHUA:
When God's Commands
Don't Make Sense,

Faith Obeys

Hebrews 11:30; Joshua 6:1-21

It was late in the game and the score was close, but Reggie Jackson knew he could steal second base. Jackson was an all-star slugger for the Baltimore Orioles and he knew the opposing pitcher had a slow move to the plate. The players had been told they did not have permission to steal unless the signal was given, and the third base coach wouldn't give Jackson the signal. But Jackson was so confident he could make it that he took off on the next pitch and slid easily into second base—safe. He dusted off his pants with an air of arrogance. In his mind, Jackson thought he had proven something to his manager, Earl Weaver.

After the game, Weaver took him aside and said, "Reggie, I knew you could steal second base, but I wanted Lee May to be able to hit behind you because he has been so effective against that pitcher. When you stole second, that left first base open and they intentionally walked Lee May. Our next batter hasn't done well against that pitcher, so I was forced to use a pinch hitter. We were left with insufficient bench strength should the game go into extra innings, which it did, and we lost." Reggie Jackson was focused on stealing a base. Earl Weaver wanted to win a game.

There are times when God's commands don't make sense. Adam and Eve didn't understand why God commanded them not to eat of the fruit of the tree in the center of the garden. That prohibition seemed unnecessary and unreasonable to them, and they disobeyed. Noah didn't fully understand why God ordered him to build a three-hundred-foot boat in his backyard, but he obeyed anyway and was saved. Samson didn't understand why God commanded him not to cut his hair. He reasoned that it didn't make any difference, and disobeyed.

We are proud people who have a hard time being submissive. When we don't understand the rationale behind God's command, it's even harder for us to obey. When God's commands don't make sense, our faith is really tested and we have the opportunity to prove whether Jesus is really Lord of our lives.

The story of Joshua's battle at Jericho is an inspiring example of what can happen when people are willing to obey God, even when His commands don't make sense.

Joshua and the Battle of Jericho

The Israelites were about to enter the land of promise. They'd wandered in the wilderness for forty years. They had been nomads for four decades. Now they were finally conditioned to be submissive and obedient to the authority of God. They were anxious to cross the Jordan and begin settling in their new homeland.

However, standing in their way were the well-fortified cities and intimidating soldiers of Canaan. Forty years earlier, these were the circumstances that had terrified their fathers, who said, "The people are like giants and we are like grasshoppers. The cities are well-fortified and they are too strong for us."

This time the people were ready to put their faith in God and follow Him. Then God gave their leader Joshua a strange command:

> Now Jericho was tightly shut up because of the Israelites. No one went out and no one came in. Then the LORD said to Joshua, "See, I have delivered Jericho into your hands, along with its king and its fighting men. March around the city

> once with all the armed men. Do this for six days. Have
> seven priests carry trumpets of rams' horns in front of the
> ark. On the seventh day, march around the city seven times,
> with the priests blowing the trumpets. When you hear them
> sound a long blast on the trumpets, have all the people give a
> loud shout; then the wall of the city will collapse and the
> people will go up, every man straight in" (Joshua 6:1-5).

These people were ready for battle. They had trained for years for this event. Now God was asking them to just march around the city? For seven days? Joshua had to be reluctant to communicate those instructions to the people. Imagine how they would respond when Joshua explained, "Here's what we're going to do: March around the city for six days and give them a show of strength, really intimidate them." O.K., Joshua, we got it. "On the seventh day, we're going to march around seven times." Seven times? Aren't we going to get worn out? "Then we'll blow our trumpets and everyone will shout, and the walls will collapse so we can march right in." Right! The people must have thought, *Where's Moses when you need him?*

The Israelites probably felt so foolish marching around the city with their women and children. I imagine the residents of Jericho staring over the wall, gawking at the Israelites, maybe even taunting them. And on that seventh day, the army must have felt silly blowing their trumpets and shouting about their victory before they had even started to fight. Obedience to this strange command required a submissive, humble, trusting spirit. But when they obeyed, look at the results:

> On the seventh day, they got up at daybreak and marched
> around the city seven times in the same manner, except that
> on that day they circled the city seven times. The seventh
> time around, when the priests sounded the trumpet blast,
> Joshua commanded the people, "Shout! For the LORD has
> given you the city!" . . . When the trumpets sounded, the

people shouted, and at the sound of the trumpet, when the people gave a loud shout, the wall collapsed; so every man charged straight in, and they took the city (Joshua 6:15, 16, 20).

Maybe God just intervened with His mighty hand and crushed the wall. He could have done that because with God all things are possible. Or maybe God knew that the wall had weakened with age and the loud noise would cause the wall to collapse. Perhaps God sent an earthquake. We don't know how He did it, but we do know that when the people shouted, the wall collapsed and the Israelites marched right in. The humble Israelites were obedient even though God's instructions seemed unreasonable, and their obedience resulted in victory.

The Lessons for Us

Like the Israelites, we are to have an obedient, submissive spirit toward God's instructions even when they don't make sense. God blesses those who walk by faith and not by sight.

God has a reason for every command

The Lord gives us instructions, not because He's a tyrant who delights in making us suffer, but because He knows what is best for us. His commands, like the owner's manual of a car, are given for our benefit so that we might have the most fulfilling life possible. John wrote, "This is love for God: to obey his commands. And his commands are not burdensome" (1 John 5:3).

Several years ago, a book was published entitled *None of These Diseases*. The author, Dr. S. I. McMillen, studied a number of the Old Testament instructions concerning diet, hygiene, and morality. In the book, he demonstrated that the Bible's commands to the Jews helped to prevent disease and promote health. There was a reason they weren't to eat pork—the risk of trichinosis was too high. There was a reason they were commanded not to eat meat that had been strangled, and not to drink blood—the risk of disease was too high. There was a reason they were to burn the clothes of a leper—the disease was contagious. And there were reasons for the prohibition against incest, homosexuality, and adultery—those activities could result in frequent venereal diseases, deformed babies, unwanted pregnancies, and broken hearts. The Jews at that time weren't medically advanced enough to understand these concepts, but God gave them diet and behavioral restrictions so they would have "none of these diseases."[17]

Years ago, two wagon trains set out simultaneously from the east coast, determined to make it to California. One group was going for gold. The other was a Christian group setting out to relocate. The Christian group stopped every first day of the week for worship and rest, while the gold rushers pressed on seven days a week. The Christian pioneers actually arrived in California first because the weekly rest commanded in Scripture made the people and the animals more efficient.

You won't always understand

All of God's commands have a purpose. "'Come now, let us reason together,' says the LORD" (Isaiah 1:18). The more we study and reason together with God, the more we understand God's ways. But we won't always understand His reasoning. Sometimes God's commands are strange. I can think of at least three reasons why we sometimes have a hard time understanding God's commands.

Our limited information. We may not have enough intelligence or information to comprehend God's rationale. As we discussed earlier, God commanded Abraham to go up to Mount Moriah and sacrifice his son Isaac. There was no way Abraham could have understood God's purpose in giving that command. He didn't know that God was going to interrupt him before the command was carried out or that God was simply testing his loyalty.

Abraham didn't know that for centuries his experience was going to be a symbol of God sacrificing His only son on Calvary. Abraham chose to obey even though he had a limited understanding.

God's desire to mature us. Harold Wilke, who was born with no arms, said that one time when he was a preschooler, he was struggling to get his shirt over his head and shoulders. He said, "I was grunting and sweating, and my mother just stood there and watched." A relative turned to his mother and said in exasperation, "Ida, why don't you help that child?" His mother responded through gritted teeth, "I am helping him." Sometimes God's commands take us through pain and struggle and we can't possibly understand at the moment that the trial is for our maturity. (See James 1:2-4.)

Sin's influence. Years ago, some Christians justified slavery in spite of the fact that Jesus commanded, "Do to others what you would have them do to you" (Matthew 7:12). They were so influenced by the accepted social customs that they couldn't see the reasoning behind the command as it related to African-Americans. Sometimes the sins of our culture have become so commonplace that our spiritual vision is impaired.

Obey anyway

A beginning pilot is taught to rely on the instrument panel when he's learning to fly. It's possible for pilots to get so jostled by a storm that they experience vertigo and lose their equilibrium. If that happens and the novice pilot can't see the horizon, he may feel he is flying level with the earth while he is actually plunging toward the ground. When in a storm, it's imperative that the pilot relies on the instrument panel and not the seat of his pants.

You can get so jostled around by the winds of false teaching that you lose your spiritual equilibrium. God's commands may seem wrong and illogical to you, but it's imperative that you put your faith in His Word—your instrument panel—and not your feelings.

Let's say your grade school child asks permission to spend the night with a friend, but you don't trust the parents of the little friend, so you say no. The child asks why and you try to give a generic answer: "I don't think you would be safe," or "I think you need to be a little older before you spend the night with someone whose parents I don't know very well." He still doesn't understand and prods you for more information. Eventually you have to say, "The answer is no because I say so. I'm the parent and you're the child. Some day you may understand, but for now you are not going because I said no." (Someone said that the hardest thing to teach a child is that "no" is a complete sentence!)

Proverbs 14:12 reads, "There is a way that seems right to a man, but in the end it leads to death." For your own good, obey God's commands even when you don't understand the rationale behind them. Your life will be blessed, your faith will be strengthened, and in time, you will grow in your understanding of God's ways.

There is a great scene in the movie, *The Karate Kid*. The teenager Daniel Larusso had asked the master karate instructor Mr. Miyagi to teach him how to defend himself. The old man put him to work waxing the car ("wax on, wax off"), sanding the floor, and painting the picket fence. The boy was obedient at first, though he had no idea why he was being asked to perform those menial tasks. He went through the motions for several days. Finally, he protested that he was being turned into a servant and wasn't being taught any karate. Then Mr. Miyagi showed him how the motions of waxing, sanding, and painting were strengthening his muscles for the motions he would use in karate. Because of his willingness to submit to Mr. Miyagi's commands, which seemed unreasonable, he was prepared to excel in karate.

God has no wasted commands. We are to be obedient students even when we don't understand His purpose. I've seen a bumper sticker that reads, "God said it, I believe it, that settles it." It sounds so dogmatic that it probably turns some people off, but that bumper sticker communicates the faith in God's authority that should typify every Christian. Someone suggested the slogan *should* read, "God said it, that settles it, whether I believe it or not!"

Some Specific Examples

Let's consider some specific commands in Scripture that sometimes seem unreasonable to us where we are required to obey by faith.

Trust Christ for salvation

Paul wrote, "For it is by grace you have been saved, through faith—and this not from yourselves, it is the gift of God—not by works, so that no one can boast" (Ephesians 2:8, 9). We are commanded to put our trust in Christ, not our good works, for salvation. That's contrary to human reason. What seems logical is that if God is just, He'll judge us by whether we're naughty or nice and all the nice people will get to go to heaven. But we're instructed that the way to heaven is through faith in what Christ did for us on the cross. That's contrary to our reasoning and human pride, but that's God's grace. His ways are not our ways.

Getting to heaven takes humility and submission, not good works. I can't boast, "I'm going to heaven when I die because I've tithed, I've been faithful to my wife, I've preached for years, I've prayed every day, I've studied the Bible." Instead, I have to be obedient to God's command, submit to Christ, and say, "I'm going to heaven when I die because I have faith in the promises of Jesus, who died for me on the cross and paid the debt for my sin. I'm trusting in Him." The songwriter Augustus Toplady wrote,

> Could my zeal no respite know,
> Could my tears forever flow,
> All for sin could not atone;
> Thou must save, and Thou alone.[18]

When we trust Christ for salvation, He commands us to be baptized into Him (Mark 16:16; Acts 2:38). Some object to that command, saying, "Water doesn't cleanse you of sin—it just gets you wet on the outside." It's such a strange ritual—dunking people in front of everybody. Some people would rather give a sizable donation, sign a card, or give a personal testimony than get dunked in front of everyone.

It's true that there's nothing magical in the water. It's possible for an insincere person to go down a dry sinner and come up a wet one. Yet God has His reasons for commanding us to be baptized: *It's a humbling act.* Jesus said, "Unless you humble yourself like a little child, you can't enter the kingdom of heaven." *It's available to all.* Baptism is free and can be received anywhere by anyone, with no economic or cultural barriers. Jesus said, "Whosoever will may come." *It's a symbol of the death, burial, and resurrection.* Baptism symbolizes that just as Christ died, was buried, and rose again, so we too have died to our sin, been buried with Christ, and been raised to walk in newness of life. Finally, *it's a testimony.* Your baptism is a witness to others of your faith.

Even if you don't understand all the reasons why God commands us to be baptized, you should do it simply because God said so. Jesus said, "If you love me, you will obey what I command" (John 14:15).

Remember the story of Naaman? (See 2 Kings 5.) He was a high-ranking soldier in the Syrian army, but Naaman had leprosy, which was a terminal disease. He went to visit the prophet Elisha, whom he had heard could perform miracles. Naaman brought expensive gifts to buy his healing. However, Elisha wouldn't even come out to see him. He sent word to Naaman to dip seven times in the Jordan River in order to be cleansed of his leprosy. Naaman's pride was wounded. He fumed, "If water would cleanse my disease, there are rivers in my home country a lot cleaner than that muddy Jordan." He rode off in a huff. He kept his pride, he kept his dignity, and he kept his leprosy.

One of the soldiers finally said to Naaman, "Sir, if the prophet had asked you to do some spectacular thing, you would have done it. Why not try this simple act?" Naaman realized his only hope was to obey the prophet. He went down into the river, taking off his garment and exposing his rotting flesh. He dipped in the river not once, but seven times as the prophet had commanded. He must have felt foolish and humbled. Second Kings 5:14 reads, "So he went down and dipped himself in the Jordan seven times, as the man of God had told him, and his flesh was restored and became clean like that of a young boy."

You might have a lot of impressive badges of rank, status, and authority. You might be proud, dignified, and influential. But underneath all of those credentials, you're diseased with sin—and it's terminal. Jesus commands, "Whoever believes and is baptized will be saved, but whoever does not believe will be condemned" (Mark 16:16). If God had asked you to do some spectacular, expensive deed, you'd do it. Are you willing, as an expression of your trust in Him, to obey when He's asked you to do something simple and humble?

Forgive those who have wronged you

Jesus commanded, "If someone strikes you on the right cheek, turn to him the other also" (Matthew 5:39). Paul wrote, "Do not take revenge, my friends, but leave room for God's wrath, for it is written: 'It is mine to avenge; I will repay,' says the Lord. On the contrary: 'If your enemy is hungry, feed him; if he is thirsty, give him something to drink' " (Romans 12:19, 20).

If someone hurts you, God commands you not to retaliate. Don't try to get back at him by injuring him, insulting him, or refusing to speak to him. You are to release him to the Lord and treat him with kindness. God will see to it that justice is meted out.

God has a reason for commanding you not to take revenge: You aren't capable of fairly administering justice. Also, when you dish out revenge, you wound yourself. Hatred eats away at your well-being. On the other hand, kindness releases anger and is good for you.

I heard Bill McCartney at a Promise Keepers rally tell an inspiring story about forgiveness. He said that a man who attended a Promise Keepers rally in Detroit had been bitter for twenty years because a former partner had intentionally cheated him out of thirty thousand dollars. He listened to the speakers talk about forgiveness and reconciliation, trying to find in his heart the ability to forgive the man who had cheated him. He had no idea that his former partner was sitting in the same arena.

A week later, the former partner came into this man's office and said, "You may not remember me, but twenty years ago, I swindled you out of thirty thousand dollars. Last week I went to a Promise Keepers rally in Detroit and really got convicted. I've come today to ask you to forgive me and to give you this check for forty thousand dollars." Both men repented of their sin—one of theft, the other of bitterness.

That's a great story, but in reality, the person who hurt us will never come back to make things right. We are commanded to forgive anyway. Jesus said, "And when you stand praying, if you hold anything against anyone, forgive him, so that your Father in heaven may forgive you your sins" (Mark 11:25). That command is so difficult to obey because it is contrary to our reasoning and instinct, but it's a test of our submission to Christ as Lord.

Love the unlovely

I heard Jim Pierson of the Christian Church Foundation for the Handicapped tell about a time he was flying from Nashville to Houston. Sitting beside him was a four-year-old girl carrying a bag that said, "Galveston Burn Center," the hospital where severe burn victims are often treated. The little girl had burns over 90 percent of her body. Her facial features—nose, lips, eyelids, and ears— were all but gone. The only place Jim could see that was not burned was a small patch of skin behind her left ear where tufts of blond hair dangled onto her shoulder. Though most of her fingers were gone, she held a coloring book and crayon in her hand.

Jim asked her to color a picture for him. She expressed a lack of self-confidence, but after some prodding, she colored a kitten. Then Jim drew a picture for her. Jim noticed the girl's mother on the other side of the aisle giving him a steely, perplexed glare. After some time passed, Jim felt moved to put his arm around the girl. Her skin felt like leather. Jim said it was so shocking that his instinct was to pull away, but he kept his arm there.

Finally, the girl's mother snapped, "Why are you talking to my daughter?"

"Well, I just wanted to talk to her," Jim responded a little defensively. "Besides, why not?"

The mother said, "My daughter was burned three years ago in a propane explosion in our home that killed her father. We've been making this same flight every month for the past three years, and you are the first person who has ever bothered to say even one word to her. Mister, why are you talking to my little girl?"

Jim said, "Ma'am, I'm a Christian, and Jesus tells me to."

Jesus said, "As I have loved you, so you must love one another" (John 13:34), "If you love me, you will obey what I command" (John 14:15), and "Whoever welcomes a little child like this in my name welcomes me" (Matthew 18:5). Anybody can show love to the beautiful, the intelligent, the sophisticated. Jesus commanded us as followers of Christ to love "the least of these."

I heard about a man who was commanded by God to go out and push a huge boulder in his backyard. The man pushed and shoved with all his might but couldn't move the boulder. He tried again the next day and the next. After several weeks of trying, he finally gave up. "Lord," he said, "I can't move this rock. It's use-less."

"I know," the Lord said, "I didn't want you to move the rock."

"Why did you tell me to push against it, then?" the man asked.

"Look how strong your arms are now!" the Lord replied. "Now, I've got another task for you."

The writer of Hebrews summarized the story of Jericho in one verse: "By faith the walls of Jericho fell, after the people had marched around them for seven days" (Hebrews 11:30). Faith in God requires us to obey commands that may not make sense to us, but our God is faithful and He promises to reward the obedient.

Wayne Nally had already mailed out his Christmas gifts—dozens of gift certificates with the message "Happy Holidays" written on them—when he came to church and listened to me preach about the meaning of Christmas. I talked about how disgusting it was that we don't even hear "Merry Christmas" anymore. People say "Happy Holidays" so they won't offend anyone by using a phrase that contains the name of Christ. I reminded the congregation that Jesus said, "If anyone is ashamed of me and my words, the Son of Man will be ashamed of him when he comes in his glory" (Luke 9:26).

Wayne was convicted. He felt like God was leading him to correct his mistake even though he hadn't intentionally been "ashamed of Christ." It cost him more than two thousand dollars, but Wayne sent everyone on his list *another* gift certificate with the message, "Merry Christmas!" I'm sure that didn't make sense to a lot of people, but Wayne was determined to do what he believed God was commanding him to do—no matter the cost. That's faith!

6

SAMSON:
When Sin Entangles,

Faith Repents

Hebrews 11:32, 34; Judges 16:4-31

A few decades ago, Bob Harrington, the "Chaplain of Bourbon Street," was a nationally known Christian leader. He was the author of several Christian books and a popular speaker. But Bob Harrington, like Samson, fell into disgrace. The pagan media was delighted to expose his downfall to the world.

Then Bob humbled himself and repented of his sins. After years of serving behind the scenes, Bob returned to the ministry. I was privileged to be present when he first asked a small group of Christian leaders if we would forgive him for what he had done and the way he had harmed the reputation of ministers. We were glad to do so and to help Bob return to the ministry.

His star may not shine as bright today and there will always be a scar, but God is using Bob again because his faith was strong enough to lead him to repentance. As Paul wrote, "Godly sorrow brings repentance that leads to salvation and leaves no regret" (2 Corinthians 7:10).

Your problems may not be as serious as Bob Harrington's were, but all of us have become entangled in sin. In the midst of your failure, you will be tempted to give up, to quit, and to believe that God could never use you again because of your past. But have faith. God is a big God and can use you despite your past failures. If you don't believe that, just look at some of the people we're studying in this book! Abraham lied about his wife (he said she was his sister to get himself out of a tight fix with Abimelech), Moses killed a man, Rahab was a prostitute, and David committed adultery.

And then there's Samson—"A he-man with a she-problem," someone called him. He's listed as one of the heroes of the faith even though most of his life was a portrait of underachievement and unrealized potential. Yet in the end, when his life had become entangled in sin, he didn't quit. In faith, he returned to God and God restored his strength.

A Privileged Man

"From everyone who has been given much, much will be demanded; and from the one who has been entrusted with much, much more will be asked" (Luke 12:48).

That verse troubles me because I have been given much. I was born in the United States of Affluence to wonderful Christian parents; I'm of sound mind and good health; I have been given a loving, supportive family; God has given me some ability to preach and has entrusted me with an incredible church. It's difficult for a person who is blessed to maintain his spiritual equilibrium. As one preacher said, "Not every man can carry a full cup." My cup runs over, which is both a wonderful blessing and an awesome responsibility.

You may know how I feel. You've been blessed to some degree by having the opportunity to live in this time period, and you were given a sound mind and good enough education that you can read this book. You can probably name many other blessings and privileges you've been given. Perhaps you've been blessed with talent, family, opportunity, or money. You know that you have a heavy responsibility to God to do more than just serve yourself.

Samson, like many of us, was a privileged man.

Born at an opportune time

In Judges 13:1 we read, "Again the Israelites did evil in the eyes of the LORD, so the LORD delivered them into the hands of the Philistines for forty years." On the surface that seems like it would have been a terrible time to be born, not an opportune time. The Israelites were so rebellious that God allowed His chosen people to be conquered by their bitter archenemies—the Philistines. The Jews were chafing under the abuse heaped on them by these ruthless barbarians. But it was an opportune time for Samson to have been born because they were craving a bold leader who could liberate them and give them hope.

We in America live in an opportune time. You might think these are terrible times with random terrorism, chaotic schools, negative media, greedy corporations, teenage gangs, rampant pornography, and anemic churches. However, this is an opportune time for Christian people, for two reasons.

There is a spiritual void. Norman Lear has a reputation for producing television programs that mock moral traditions, but he wrote a newspaper article in which he said, "We're in need of a spiritual revival" and urged Americans to dialogue over our common spiritual life in this desolate age.[19] Even secular producers and politicians recognize that something is seriously wrong. They are pleading for a return to basic values. Money, education, laws, and prisons can't restrain the evil in men's hearts. Only the gospel of Christ changes someone's heart. This is an opportune time for the church to impact the world for Jesus Christ. The darker the cave, the more valuable the flashlight! Jesus said, "You are the light of the world. A city on a hill cannot be hidden" (Matthew 5:14).

There is advanced technology. I can be a thousand miles from home, walk up to a machine, slip in a card, punch in a couple of numbers, and, in less than one minute, have some cash in my hands! And I get a receipt with the balance of my checking account in a bank located a thousand miles away! We're living in an era of computers, communication satellites, mobile phones, and jet travel. Never before in history could the gospel of Christ make the kind of worldwide impact that it can today. My friend Russ Summay sits at his computer several times each month and communicates through the Internet with his friends who are missionaries thousands of miles away. Our church's Web site (www.southeastchristian.org) now broadcasts our weekly sermons over the Internet. Anyone in the world with the right kind of computer and a phone line can hear the gospel being preached.

We have been given the resources to make a difference for Christ in our era. We should be "making the most of every opportunity, because the days are evil" (Ephesians 5:16). Like Samson, we are living in a time when we are surrounded by evil. Yet with God as our strength, we should see this as an opportunity. This is a time for expanded ministries, bold witnesses, courageous preachers, strong churches, and gigantic plans. This is a time for great faith! "To whom much is given, much is required."

Raised by godly parents

Samson was also privileged to be raised by godly parents.

> A certain man of Zorah, named Manoah, from the clan of the Danites, had a wife who was sterile and remained childless. The angel of the LORD appeared to her and said, "You are sterile and childless, but you are going to conceive and have a son. Now see to it that you drink no wine or other fermented drink and that you do not eat anything unclean" (Judges 13:2-4).

They were childless, but faithful to God. When couples want children but cannot have them, their faith in God is tested. Some can grow bitter and rebellious against God because He doesn't answer their prayers as they wish He would. Manoah and his wife were disappointed, but they still trusted God.

They were given a promise and believed God's word. When Abraham's elderly wife Sarah was told she would have a baby, she laughed. When the angel of the Lord told Manoah's wife she would conceive, she believed it without questioning. Her husband believed it, too, and his first response was to pray for spiritual guidance in their parenting. "Then Manoah prayed to the LORD: 'O Lord, I beg you, let the man of God you sent to us come again to teach us how to bring up the boy who is to be born'" (Judges 13:8). The angel did return, and Samson's parents were able to receive specific instructions about how to raise this special boy.

They obeyed God's difficult commands. The angel told Manoah's wife that her son must be a "Nazirite, set apart to God from birth" (Judges 13:5). Numbers 6:3-7 outlines three strict disciplines required of a Nazirite.

First, *a Nazirite was not to cut his hair*, symbolizing separation from the pride of appearance. No razor should come upon his head. His consecration to God was not concealed. It was unusual for a boy to have long hair, so a Nazirite was a marked man, easily distinguishable in any company.

Second, *a Nazirite had to abstain from any contact with a dead body*. Death is the fruit of sin, and touching a dead body in Jewish law made a man unclean.

Third, *a Nazirite was to abstain from wine*, symbolizing his separation from sensual pleasures. He was to be distinctive. There wasn't even to be a hint of worldliness.

It would be difficult to raise a Nazirite child. It would require constant diligence on the part of Manoah and his wife to follow through with those rigid rules. I can just hear Samson as a child questioning his parents: "Why can't I pick up that dead snake? Other kids can!" "All the other kids can drink wine, Mom. I can handle it." "The kids make fun of my long hair. Please let me get it cut!" But Samson's parents stayed the course. They must have explained over and over that Samson was a special child of God, sanctified, and therefore he was not to act like the other children.

My parents raised me to be distinctive as a Christian. When I became a teenager, I wanted to be popular with the other kids. Then when I was fourteen years old, a terrible thing happened. Our physical education teacher decided we needed a little culture, so for six weeks he taught dance lessons in gym class.

My parents believed that Christians shouldn't dance, so they sent a note to my teacher explaining that I would not be allowed to participate. The teacher sat a Mennonite boy and me on the stage where we watched the others receiving dance lessons. My friends asked, "Russell, why aren't you out here?" I had to say, "It's against my religion." I felt awkward, rejected, and different, and I didn't like it. So I started making fun of them. The next week, four other kids had notes from their parents saying it was against their religion to dance. The teacher decided we should go to study hall instead of sitting on the stage.

Nobody likes to be different. I imagine Samson had a hard time as a child with that Nazirite vow and it was probably a constant hassle for his parents, but they stuck with it.

Given special strength

Samson is best remembered for his physical strength. There is a brand of luggage called Samsonite® because the name "Samson" still communicates durability and strength. The Bible says that Samson "grew and the LORD blessed him, and the Spirit of the LORD began to stir him" (Judges 13:24, 25). God was ready to use Samson's special strength in a mighty way.

As we will see shortly, Samson suffered greatly because he forgot the source of his strength and began putting faith in his own abilities. Contrary to his parents' wishes, Samson became friendly with the enemies of the Israelites. Samson began dating Philistine women. The Bible says, "Bad company corrupts good character" (1 Corinthians 15:33), and Samson's association with the enemy was eventually his downfall.

For twenty years, Samson's occasional feats of strength saved

Israel from complete domination by the Philistines and reminded them of their ultimate hope. Samson killed a lion with his bare hands, killed thirty Philistines in Ashkelon, killed a thousand Philistines with the jawbone of a donkey, and performed many other miraculous feats of strength.

What do you think Samson looked like? We usually picture a guy with an impressive build, like Arnold Schwarzenegger or The Rock. Some commentators have pointed out that Samson probably wasn't very impressive-looking at all because people were always questioning how Samson could do such mighty things. They didn't say, "He's strong because he's got such gigantic muscles." Instead they asked, "What's the secret of his strength?" His great strength came from some miraculous source besides his body.

I know one teacher who tells his Sunday school class that Samson probably looked like Barney Fife! I don't know if he was that skinny, but people were convinced Samson had miraculous power and not just a superhuman body. J. Oswald Sanders, in his book, *Spiritual Manpower*, wrote,

> A careful reading of the narrative makes it clear that [Samson's] great strength did not lie in gigantic stature or bulging muscles. . . . Why would Delilah and the Philistines be puzzled about the source of his great strength if it was physically obvious? He himself told her that he would be "like any other man" (Judges 16:17) if his hair was cut.[20]

Samson's strength was not in his hair or in his bulk, but in his God.

When you are extremely gifted—whether in business, entertainment, education, athletics, music, or physical appearance—it's important to recognize that God is the author of your strength. Your gifts are to be used for His glory and not your own. Deep down you know your gifts are given from God, not something you've acquired by your own effort. You may have worked hard to polish your talents, but if you hadn't been gifted from the beginning, all of your efforts would have been fruitless. Regardless of your area of giftedness, you will face the temptation to exploit what God has given you for your own glory instead of His. Don't fall into the same trap that Samson did. Maintain your faith in God and keep your pride under control.

A Fallen Man

Although Samson sometimes provided glimpses of hope for his people, he never realized his potential. J. Oswald Sanders calls him "the champion who became a clown."[21] He never raised an army, never won a battle, and never rallied the men of Israel to his side. In the end, he was exploited and ridiculed by his enemies as a buffoon. And the reason Samson's life ended in tragedy can be summed up in one word—pride. Samson's ego was the source of his downfall. He thought too highly of himself. He felt superior to all those around him, including God. The result for Samson was not so much a spectacular fall off a cliff, but more of a gradual slide down the slippery slope of sin. The Bible says that some Old Testament events are written down as warnings for us (1 Corinthians 10:11). Samson's disastrous end should serve as a warning to us: Don't become arrogant, egotistical, and self-sufficient. "Pride goes before destruction, a haughty spirit before a fall" (Proverbs 16:18). Notice several ways Samson's pride got him into trouble.

He was too proud to be satisfied with Hebrew women

God had given clear instructions to the Israelites that they were not to intermarry with unbelievers (Deuteronomy 7:3). Samson lived in a time of wickedness, and intermarriage with pagans may have been quite common. Maybe the Jews boasted of their tolerance toward other religions and scoffed at the old restrictions their fathers had handed down to them.

Samson's father was from the tribe of Dan, which was right on the border of Philistine territory. Dan was where the young men assembled for military training. Just as the nightspots are popular on the highway leading to a military base, the wicked pleasures of Timnah lay near the camp of Dan. The Bible says, "Samson went down to Timnah and saw there a young Philistine woman" (Judges 14:1).

Samson had an eye for attractive women, and the Philistine women were flashier and more daring than the Hebrews. One Christian philosopher said, "The grass always looks greener on the other side of the fence. But it's poison. God has put the fence there to protect us." Samson refused to realize God's fence was there for a reason.

There was an article in *Fortune* magazine a few years ago titled, "The Trophy Wife Is Back With Brains." The article read,

> Powerful men are beginning to demand trophy wives. The more money men make, the argument goes, the more self-assured they become, and the easier it is for them to think, "I deserve a queen." Enter the second wife: a decade or two younger than her husband, sometimes several inches taller, beautiful and very often accomplished.
>
> "The culture of self-indulgence has just crept up to the CEO level," says Boston psychologist Harry Levinson, a longtime counselor to top management people. "Indulgence is an issue for people who have worked very hard to get where they are. They feel they've earned it, they're entitled to it."[22]

I asked our Saturday morning men's Bible study why older men marry younger women. One guy quipped, "So they'll have someone to drive them at night!" In most cases, the issue is pride, and it is no laughing matter. In the wake of their self-indulgent actions lie broken families, shattered dreams, and bitterness. One day they will wake up and wonder how they could have been so foolish.

Scripture says, "When pride comes, then comes disgrace, but with humility comes wisdom" (Proverbs 11:2).

He was too proud to listen to the counsel of his parents

> When he returned, he said to his father and mother, "I have seen a Philistine woman in Timnah; now get her for me as my wife." His father and mother replied, "Isn't there an acceptable woman among your relatives or among all our people? Must you go to the uncircumcised Philistines to get a wife?" But Samson said to his father, "Get her for me. She's the right one for me" (Judges 14:2, 3).

Samson was too egotistical to listen to his mom and dad. He felt superior to his parents. He thought, *What do they know about dating and hormones? They're naive.*

There are three stages of maturity through which every child develops: dependence, independence, and interdependence. A little baby is completely *dependent* upon his parents for support and life. A teenager reaches a stage of *independence* where he tries to prove he doesn't need Mom and Dad at all. The third stage is *interdependence*, where the grown child realizes for the first time that he and his parents need each other. Somebody described the stages of life this way:

- Ages 2-5—Dad knows everything.
- Ages 6-9—Dad knows most things.
- Ages 10-12—Dad knows some things.
- Ages 13-19—Dad knows nothing.
- Ages 20-29—Dad knows some things.
- Ages 30-39—Dad knows most things.
- Ages 40-50—Better check with Dad.
- Ages 50 and up—Dad used to say.

Proverbs 13:10 says, "Pride only breeds quarrels, but wisdom is found in those who take advice." Proud Samson argued with his parents and insisted on marrying the Philistine girl, so they reluctantly agreed and everyone planned a big wedding party. But the party—and the relationship—turned out to be a disaster.

The customary bachelor party lasted seven days. Samson and his thirty groomsmen (all Philistines) set about partying for the week. Samson thought he'd have some fun with the groomsmen, so he told them a riddle. Along the way to his girlfriend's house, Samson had come upon a lion, which he proceeded to kill with his bare hands. The next time he traveled the road, he went to check on the carcass of the dead lion and saw that some honeybees had made a hive in the carcass. Samson reached into the beehive and grabbed some honey for himself and his parents. (Never mind that as a Nazirite, Samson was not to touch the body of a dead animal! You can see that his values were already beginning to slip.) So Samson made up the following riddle for his Philistine companions: "Out of the eater, something to eat; out of the strong, something sweet" (Judges 14:14).

He told the Philistines that if they could figure out the riddle by the wedding night, he'd give them each a new set of clothes. If they couldn't figure it out, they owed him thirty new sets of clothes. The thirty groomsmen agreed and set about trying to discover the riddle. They went straight to Samson's fiancée, who got offended that Samson hadn't told her the answer to the riddle. The Scriptures say she cried the whole seven days, saying, "You hate me! You don't really love me. You've given my people a riddle, but you haven't told me the answer" (Judges 14:16). Samson finally gave into her nagging and told her the story, which she proceeded to tell Samson's companions.

> Before sunset on the seventh day the men of the town said to him, "What is sweeter than honey? What is stronger than a lion?" Samson said to them, "If you had not plowed with my heifer, you would not have solved my riddle." Then the Spirit of the LORD came upon him in power. He went down to

> Ashkelon, struck down thirty of their men, stripped them of
> their belongings and gave their clothes to those who had
> explained the riddle. Burning with anger, he went up to his
> father's house. And Samson's wife was given to the friend
> who had attended him at his wedding (Judges 14:18-20).

When Samson realized he'd been betrayed, he went back home
for a few days to stay with his parents where he was loved and
treated with respect. All of a sudden, Mom and Dad were smarter
than he had thought and home wasn't such a bad place after all.

All this humiliation could have been avoided if Samson had
just listened to his parents. "A fool spurns his father's discipline,
but whoever heeds correction shows prudence" (Proverbs 15:5).

A few years ago in a nearby county, four teenagers sneaked out
of their homes in the middle of the night and went for a joyride in
one of their parents' Mercedes convertible. The driver of the car
was fifteen years old, which is below the legal driving age in
Kentucky. The youngest of the four was just thirteen. At 3 A.M.,
there was a terrible crash and all four of the teens were killed. If
you are a parent, your heart breaks when you hear that story
because you can imagine how the parents of those four teenagers
must have felt. How those parents wish their children had accepted their guidelines and not been so full of rebellious pride.

He was too proud to accept
the consequences of his actions

After a cooling-down period, Samson decided to return to
Timnah to get his wife. The girl's father explained that he thought
Samson was gone for good, so he had given the bride to the best
man. Samson again was furious. He said, "This time I have a right
to get even with the Philistines; I will really harm them" (Judges
15:3).

What Samson should have done at that point was repent. He
should have humbled himself before God and said, "Lord, I've

been spiritually drifting for many years. I disregarded the counsel of Moses and attempted to marry a Philistine girl. I disdained the instructions of my godly parents who counseled me wisely. I even violated my Nazirite vow by touching a dead body and participating in the feasts with the Philistines. Now I've gotten burned because I played with fire. I'm reaping what I sowed. Please forgive me, Lord, and lead me in paths everlasting."

When King David made that kind of confession after his sin with Bathsheba, God wiped the slate clean and allowed David to remain in power. But it took a humble admission of failure on David's part—an admission Samson wasn't yet willing to make. Instead of humbling himself, Samson sought revenge. There's a Chinese proverb that says, "Whoever seeks revenge should first dig two graves." A vengeful spirit will kill you.

> So he went out and caught three hundred foxes and tied them tail to tail in pairs. He then fastened a torch to every pair of tails, lit the torches and let the foxes loose in the standing grain of the Philistines. He burned up the shocks and standing grain, together with the vineyards and olive groves. When the Philistines asked, "Who did this?" they were told, "Samson, the Timnite's son-in-law, because his wife was given to his friend." So the Philistines went up and burned her and her father to death. Samson said to them, "Since you've acted like this, I won't stop until I get my revenge on you." He attacked them viciously and slaughtered many of them. Then he went down and stayed in a cave in the rock of Etam (Judges 15:4-8).

J. Oswald Sanders said of Samson, "He was moved more by . . . a desire for personal vengeance than by true patriotism—a solitary man waging his conflict alone. It was not only after he lost his sight that he acted the buffoon!"[23]

Paul said in Romans 12:19, "Do not take revenge, my friends, but leave room for God's wrath, for it is written: 'It is mine to avenge; I will repay,' says the Lord." Faith believes that God will make all things right in the end, but ego insists on settling the score personally and immediately rather than waiting for God's justice.

"No one ever treats me like that and gets away with it. I don't get mad, I get even!" Those are expressions of a proud person, and they were the expressions of Samson. Proverbs says, "A fool gives full vent to his anger, but a wise man keeps himself under control" (Proverbs 29:11).

Do you know what surprises me? God didn't quit on Samson. Samson's fellow Jews tied him up and handed him over to the Philistines to appease the anger of their enemies after Samson had destroyed so many of their men. But Samson broke loose and killed another thousand Philistines using the jawbone of a donkey. Afterwards, he was so exhausted and thirsty that he sat down and complained to God: "You have given your servant this great victory. Must I now die of thirst and fall into the hands of the uncircumcised?" (Judges 15:18). If I had been God, I would have struck the ungrateful man dead right then. But the Bible says, "Then God opened up the hollow place in Lehi, and water came out of it. When Samson drank, his strength returned and he revived. So the spring was called En Hakkore, and it is still there in Lehi" (Judges 15:19). God's patience is amazing. He gives people chance after chance to repent. Samson lived in selfishness and semidisobedience for twenty years, yet God kept empowering him.

He was too proud to see the danger ahead

Someone said, "We treat God like a policeman. When we're going 65 mph in a 40-mph zone, we don't want to see Him. But when someone is trying to break into our house at 2 A.M., we want Him right there! Samson cried out to God for help when he was dying of thirst, but when his thirst was satisfied, it wasn't long before he didn't want God around.

> One day Samson went to Gaza, where he saw a prostitute.
> He went in to spend the night with her. The people of Gaza
> were told, "Samson is here!" So they surrounded the place
> and lay in wait for him all night at the city gate. They made
> no move during the night, saying, "At dawn we'll kill him."
> But Samson lay there only until the middle of the night.
> Then he got up and took hold of the doors of the city gate,
> together with the two posts, and tore them loose, bar and all.
> He lifted them to his shoulders and carried them to the top
> of the hill that faces Hebron (Judges 16:1-3).

Hebron is forty miles from Gaza! Samson uprooted the huge
gate from its foundations, and it was discovered a few days later,
forty miles away. The Philistines were terrified of this Rambo-like
creature. And Samson was becoming more and more convinced
that he was someone special in his own power. He had mocked
God again by spending the night with a Philistine prostitute, but
God remained patient.

Then along came Delilah, the Philistine woman who would
finally cause Samson's downfall.

> Some time later, he fell in love with a woman in the Valley of
> Sorek whose name was Delilah. The rulers of the Philistines
> went to her and said, "See if you can lure him into showing
> you the secret of his great strength and how we can overpow-
> er him so we may tie him up and subdue him. Each one of
> us will give you eleven hundred shekels of silver" (Judges
> 16:4, 5).

Eleven hundred shekels of silver was a huge reward. Remember
that Joseph had been sold by his brothers for just twenty shekels.
If she could subdue Samson, she'd be rich. Delilah slept with
Samson and begged him to tell her the secret of his strength.

At first Samson toyed with her, telling her, "Tie me with seven
strips of leather and I become as weak as any man." Delilah tried

it soon thereafter, with Philistine men hidden in the next room. But Samson shredded the leather strips and his secret was not discovered.

Delilah was hurt. "You lied to me!" she cried. Never mind that she had betrayed his secret. You'd think that Samson would get the message that this girl was going to take away his strength if she could. He should have fled like Joseph did from Potiphar's wife. Yet Samson arrogantly thought he could play with fire without getting burned.

Samson said, "O.K., O.K. Here's the truth: Tie me with new ropes and I can't break them." Sure enough, Delilah tried it and Samson broke free of the ropes.

Delilah again cried her crocodile tears and said, "You're making a fool of me!"

Samson said, "All right, here's the truth: Tie my long locks of hair in a weaver's loom and I'll become as weak as any other man."

Samson was now flirting with the truth—he was talking about his long hair. He was tiptoeing on the spider's web, seeing how close he could come to disaster without getting caught.

> So while he was sleeping, Delilah took the seven braids of his head, wove them into the fabric and tightened it with the pin. Again she called to him, "Samson, the Philistines are upon you!" He awoke from his sleep and pulled up the pin and the loom, with the fabric. Then she said to him, "How can you say, 'I love you,' when you won't confide in me? This is the third time you have made a fool of me and haven't told me the secret of your great strength." With such nagging she prodded him day after day until he was tired to death (Judges 16:13-16).

Is Samson stupid or what? When a person drifts from God, he loses all sense of reason. Why did Samson act this way? Maybe he had gotten by with disobeying God for so long, he thought cutting his hair wouldn't matter. God hadn't take away his strength when he had touched a dead body or drank wine or slept with a prostitute. Maybe Samson began to believe he really was that strong on his own, that God would never take away his strength. Or maybe Samson was just so in *lust* that he lost all sense of reason.

In his book, *A Look at Life From a Deer Stand*, Steve Chapman tells of sitting quietly in a tree stand hoping to spot a deer. Suddenly, he heard a crashing sound coming through the woods near him. His adrenaline starting rushing as he quickly pulled his rifle to his shoulder and slipped off the safety. Soon he spotted a doe bounding across in front of him, followed by a buck chasing after her. Deer have extremely keen senses of smell, sight, and hearing. They are normally spooked by the slightest sound, except during mating season. Steve was only forty yards away, and he took aim with his 30.06 rifle. He missed—twice—but his shots went unnoticed by the deer! Steve said, "I could have been playing the piano in that tree stand and it wouldn't have mattered to that buck."

A few moments later, he heard another crashing sound from the opposite direction, and behold, here they came again—the same two deer—running toward him! Steve said,

> I couldn't believe it. It occurred to me that the old buck might not have known or even cared that I was there but, hey, that doe must have known. I kind of think she was bringing him back by me. "Bless her heart! She's giving me another chance," I said to myself. In fact, I do believe I heard a female voice as they were crashing through the second time screaming, "Shoot him! Shoot him!"

Steve missed again twice and the two deer disappeared. Steve didn't get his deer, but he did get this moral from his experience:

> Though acting on instinct, that buck had cast aside its normal self-protective use of his big ears and keen sense of smell.

All that was crucial for his survival in the wild was traded for a chase. A deer's "rut" or mating season lasts four or five weeks of the year, and it is not unusual for the white-tailed buck to act crazy during this period. He may have been acting normal, but in regards to his own safety and his usual overly cautious nature, he was acting like a fool. The bottom line is that while in "rut," a buck sure makes an easy target of himself.[24]

Men (and women) act just as crazy. A man can lose all common sense, endanger his spiritual life, and bound into dangerous territory, risking all that is important to him, for a few moments of physical pleasure. Samson had lost all sense of reason. He should have fled, but his lust consumed his common sense.

The Scriptures record the tragedy in one phrase: "So he told her everything."

"No razor has ever been used on my head," he said, "because I have been a Nazirite set apart to God since birth. If my head were shaved, my strength would leave me, and I would become as weak as any other man" (Judges 16:17). Somehow Delilah knew he had finally told her the truth.

> When Delilah saw that he had told her everything, she sent word to the rulers of the Philistines, "Come back once more; he has told me everything." So the rulers of the Philistines returned with the silver in their hands. Having put him to sleep on her lap, she called a man to shave off the seven braids of his hair, and so began to subdue him. And his strength left him. Then she called, "Samson, the Philistines are upon you!" (Judges 16:18-20).

What follows is one of the saddest verses in the Bible: "He awoke from his sleep and thought, 'I'll go out as before and shake myself free.' But he did not know that the LORD had left him" (Judges 16:20).

You can toy with God's grace too long. Eventually even God's patience runs out. The Bible says, "If we deliberately keep on sinning after we have received the knowledge of the truth, no sacrifice for sins is left, but only a fearful expectation of judgment and of raging fire that will consume the enemies of God" (Hebrews 10:26, 27).

When he awoke, Samson still felt the same as he always had, but his power was gone. When he tried to ward off the Philistines, his blows bounced off of them. He fought them as if he were in a bad dream, in slow motion, unable to gather the strength he once knew. The Philistines started beating him up, taunting and torturing him, and Samson was helpless. "Then the Philistines seized him, gouged out his eyes and took him down to Gaza. Binding him with bronze shackles, they set him to grinding in the prison" (Judges 16:21).

Galatians 6:7, 8 reads, "Do not be deceived: God cannot be mocked. A man reaps what he sows. The one who sows to please his sinful nature, from that nature will reap destruction; the one who sows to please the Spirit, from the Spirit will reap eternal life."

Satan is ruthless. The payment he requires for the pleasures of sin is always exorbitant. He delights in mocking God's people. There's an old sermon outline about Samson: Sin blinds, sin binds, and sin grinds.

A Repentant Man

Judges 16:22 reads, "But the hair on his head began to grow again after it had been shaved." In prison, Samson began to realize the mess he had made of his life. He began to see the wasted potential, the misused talent, and the missed opportunities. Samson was finally humbled. He began to petition God for one last opportunity to defeat the Philistines.

The Philistines threw a party to celebrate their victory over Samson. In their temple they praised their false god for giving them victory. "While they were in high spirits, they shouted, 'Bring out Samson to entertain us' " (Judges 16:25). Samson was brought out and put between the two pillars of the temple, and the Bible says, "He performed for them." They must have mocked him and demanded that he perform some humiliating act. In the past, Samson would have proudly thumped his enemies without ever recognizing the God who had given him strength. This time, humbled by his circumstances, Samson petitioned his God for grace and help.

> Samson said to the servant who held his hand, "Put me where I can feel the pillars that support the temple, so that I may lean against them." Now the temple was crowded with men and women; all the rulers of the Philistines were there, and on the roof were about three thousand men and women watching Samson perform. Then Samson prayed to the LORD, "O Sovereign LORD, remember me. O God, please strengthen me just once more, and let me with one blow get revenge on the Philistines for my two eyes." Then Samson reached toward the two central pillars on which the temple stood. Bracing himself against them, his right hand on the one and his left hand on the other, Samson said, "Let me die with the Philistines!" Then he pushed with all his might, and down came the temple on the rulers and all the people in it. Thus he killed many more when he died than while he lived (Judges 16:26-30).

Samson finally recognized the source of his strength and put his faith in the God who had empowered him. There's a clear message for us: Regardless of your past, regardless of the commitments you've broken, the people you've hurt, or the consequences you've suffered, God is still waiting for you to repent, to turn back, to ask for forgiveness. And if you will again put your faith in God, He will restore you.

Annie[25] is a friend of ours and a faithful member of our church. A few years ago, Annie took a bold step of faith. She was a

Christian at the time, but she had a secret alcohol addiction. Annie covered over her addiction so well that her *husband* didn't even know she drank. After an automobile accident and several other close calls, she decided it was time to come clean. She confessed her secret to her husband, repented before God, and began to put her life back together. Annie prayed that God would help her overcome her addiction and she began attending Alcoholics Anonymous meetings *every day.*

Annie has remained sober for years and is now a faithful employee on our church staff. She continues to go to AA meetings regularly and witness for Christ in that arena. Annie discovered that people who come to AA meetings are searching for a place to belong and spiritual guidance, so she began to befriend them and introduce them to Christ. She has invited dozens of her friends from AA to visit our church and has helped to bring them to the Lord.

God told the people of Israel that if they repented of their sins, He would repay them "for the years the locusts have eaten" (Joel 2:25). Maybe because of your sin, the locusts have eaten away many years of your life. It's not too late to turn back. Recognize the source of your strength, and have faith that God can and will restore the years the locusts have eaten.

There's a proverb that says, "No matter how far you've traveled on the wrong road, turn back." It's not too late. If you will petition God to forgive you of your sins and of the wasted years, He will forgive you. The Bible says, "If we confess our sins, he is faithful and just and will forgive us our sins and purify us from all unrighteousness" (1 John 1:9).

And just as He did with Samson and with Annie, God just may return your strength to you and use you in an even mightier way than you ever dreamed.

7

SAMUEL:
When God Calls,
Faith Answers

Hebrews 11:32, 33; 1 Samuel 1, 3

A few years ago, some friends gave me a great book titled *Growing Up Born Again: A Whimsical Look at the Blessings and Tribulations of Growing Up Born Again.* It's a humorous but touching reminder of the common experiences of those of us who have grown up in church. According to the authors, if you grew up born again:

- You attended church every Sunday morning and youth group on Sunday night.
- You went to Christian camp and VBS in the summer.
- Your home wasn't cluttered with ashtrays and lewd pictures; instead, you had a print of Sallman's "Head of Christ" on the wall and a plaque that read, "As for me and my house, we will serve the Lord."
- Instead of *True Confessions* magazines on the coffee table, there were *Moody Monthly* or *Decision* magazines.
- You memorized the books of the Bible and had perfect attendance pins.
- You knew all the songs: "Do Lord," "Heavenly Sunshine," "Behold, Behold, I Stand at the Door and Knock, Knock, Knock," and "I'm in the Lord's Army."
- You learned to play an instrument so that one day you could be "of service to the Lord" by accompanying hymns

or playing the offertory during the service.

- You learned that acceptable instruments were the piano, flute, and violin, and doubtful instruments were the drums, saxophone, and electric guitar.
- You knew the church lingo: "love offering," "covered dish supper," "sword drill," "red-letter edition," "backslide," "under conviction," "unspoken request," and "all God's people said . . . Amen!"[26]

If you grew up in a Christian home, there are some advantages, for which you should be thankful, and some dangers. The advantages far outweigh the disadvantages, but we need to be conscious of both. The judge and prophet Samuel is a helpful example of a man who grew up in a spiritual setting and faithfully answered God's call from the time that he was a young boy.

Samuel's Spiritual Advantages

A godly home

Like Samson, Samuel also had the blessing of God-fearing parents. Samuel's father, Elkanah, was a believer, but the Bible tells us more about his mother, Hannah. She was an unselfish, devout worshiper of God. For a number of years, she was barren and prayed daily that God would give her a son.

> In bitterness of soul Hannah wept much and prayed to the LORD. And she made a vow, saying, "O LORD Almighty, if you will only look upon your servant's misery and remember me, and not forget your servant but give her a son, then I will give him to the LORD for all the days of his life, and no razor will ever be used on his head" (1 Samuel 1:10, 11).

Hannah promised God that if she could have a son, she would give him back to the Lord as His special servant.

So in the course of time Hannah conceived and gave birth to a son. She named him Samuel, saying, "Because I asked the LORD for him." When the man Elkanah went up with all his family to offer the annual sacrifice to the LORD and to fulfill his vow, Hannah did not go. She said to her husband, "After the boy is weaned, I will take him and present him before the LORD, and he will live there always" (1 Samuel 1:20-22).

When Samuel was old enough to live apart from his mother, she brought him to the tabernacle and left him there permanently. Some commentators suggest that he was two years old, others say he may have been as old as four or five. Most of us have a difficult time sending our children off to college when they're eighteen. Hannah willed her child to God when he was still a toddler. The Bible says, "Each year his mother made him a little robe and took it to him when she went up with her husband to offer the annual sacrifice" (1 Samuel 2:19).

Imagine Hannah at home, thinking about her son, sewing the robe she would take to him when she visited the temple for the annual sacrifice. As she worked, she probably estimated how much he had grown since the last time she saw him. It must have been so difficult for Hannah, but she believed that to see her son answer God's call was more important than her natural desire to keep him close to her.

It's a tremendous spiritual advantage to have godly parents. If you grew up in a Christian home and your parents took you to church regularly, taught you Bible stories, and imparted basic spiritual values to you by word and example, then you are greatly blessed. Be grateful. You have probably been protected from some of the more heinous temptations and problems to which others are subjected. And you understand right and wrong almost instinctively. Knowing and following the Lord come much easier to you because of your background.

A godly mentor

Samuel was also privileged to have a godly mentor, Eli, the high priest of Israel. He was an imperfect man. Scripture records that he was vastly overweight and apparently wasn't a very good father to his two sons who were "wicked men" (1 Samuel 2:12). But Eli loved the Lord and faithfully mentored Samuel. He trained Samuel to be a minister of God (1 Samuel 2:18), and when the time was right, Eli encouraged Samuel to be sensitive to God's call even though Samuel would be replacing Eli's own sons in the priesthood.

If you grew up in the church, you can probably recall influential spiritual mentors who made a significant difference in your life—Sunday school teachers, youth leaders, ministers, evangelists, musicians, family friends, or missionaries. Those people modeled the Christian life for you, nurtured you, cared for you, and encouraged you to be faithful to the Lord. You knew them well enough to know they were imperfect, but they still loved the Lord.

My mother would never let me play ball on Sunday, "the Lord's Day." Then a new preacher, Harry Orn, came to our church. Brother Harry was an outstanding athlete. He was the all-county catcher in the county baseball league. That impressed me. And then I discovered that sometimes Harry played baseball on *Sunday!* In fact, I'm confident that there were times he wore his baseball uniform under his suit so he could more easily get to a one o'clock baseball game. When my mother would tell me I couldn't play baseball on Sundays, I'd protest, "But Mom, Brother Harry plays baseball on Sunday." She'd say, "Brother Harry does some other things I don't approve of, too." I knew my parents loved Brother Harry and respected him, but they didn't think he was perfect. That made me like him all the more.

Sometimes people who come to Christ later in life expect too much of their spiritual leaders, and they become disillusioned when they discover their mentors have feet of clay. One of the advantages of growing up in the church is that you have learned that Christian people are imperfect; only Christ is perfect. Samuel had grown to respect Eli as a godly mentor, but he also knew Eli's weaknesses and didn't expect perfection.

A godly place

Samuel also grew up in a godly place—the tabernacle. If you are the child of a minister or dedicated church officer, you probably grew up thinking the church building was your second home. Maybe you even lived in a parsonage right next door to the church. Samuel literally grew up living *in* the church building.

When I was growing up, I spent many hours at church. I watched people prepare communion, fill the baptistry, and wash the robes. I helped fold the bulletins. I stood behind the pulpit after church and fingered the pulpit Bible and read the preacher's notes. I was exposed to missionaries, Bible college presidents, evangelists, and famous Christian singers traveling through our town. They not only spoke at our church, they ate in our home and slept in our beds because my parents always opened up our home to those who were traveling through.

There's a great advantage to growing up in church, but there's also an inherent danger: You can become so familiar with the sacred that it loses its wonder for you.

A couple of years ago, I read that the North Carolina State Medical Board had suspended the license of a neurosurgeon in Wilmington, North Carolina. An investigation had revealed that in the middle of a surgery, while a patient's brain was exposed, the neurosurgeon left the operating room for twenty-five minutes to take a lunch break. No other physician was present to care for the patient. In another case, the surgeon had instructed an untrained nurse to drill holes in a patient's head and begin work on the outer brain. When a person regularly deals with an awesome responsibility, he's tempted to become too casual.

Eli's sons, Hophni and Phinehas, fell to that temptation. They were responsible for taking care of the sacrifices people brought to the tabernacle. It became so common to them that instead of following God's instructions, they regularly ate some of the meat that was improper for them to eat and committed adultery with some of the women who served at the entrance of the tabernacle. The Bible says, "They were treating the LORD's offering with contempt" (2 Samuel 2:17).

Some of the greatest spiritual leaders are people who grew up in godly homes. On the other hand, some of the most sacrilegious people in the world are preachers' kids! They've lost their sense of respect for the sacred. If you grew up "born again," you have to maintain vigilance and never lose the sense of wonder at the awesomeness of God. We read of Samuel, "And the boy Samuel continued to grow in stature and in favor with the LORD and with men" (1 Samuel 2:26).

Samuel's Personal Encounter With God

Samuel was privileged to have a personal encounter with God at a young age. We read in 1 Samuel 3:

> The boy Samuel ministered before the LORD under Eli. In those days the word of the LORD was rare; there were not many visions. One night Eli, whose eyes were becoming so weak that he could barely see, was lying down in his usual place. The lamp of God had not yet gone out, and Samuel was lying down in the temple of the LORD, where the ark of God was. Then the LORD called Samuel. Samuel answered, "Here I am." And he ran to Eli and said, "Here I am; you called me." But Eli said, "I did not call; go back and lie down." So he went and lay down (1 Samuel 3:1-5).

Samuel was very young when this happened. Josephus, the Jewish historian, says he was about twelve years old when the

Lord called him. What an awesome experience this would have been! The Scripture says that the word of the Lord was rare in those days. It wasn't common for God to reveal himself or speak directly to people. Samuel was probably used to Eli calling him in the middle of the night because the old man was blind. But when Samuel ran to him, Eli said, "I didn't call you. Go back to bed."

> Again the LORD called, "Samuel!" And Samuel got up and went to Eli and said, "Here I am; you called me." "My son," Eli said, "I did not call; go back and lie down." Now Samuel did not yet know the LORD: The word of the LORD had not yet been revealed to him (1 Samuel 3:6, 7).

"Samuel did not yet know the Lord." Just because you grow up with godly parents and godly mentors in a godly place doesn't mean you know the Lord. You can be in church all your life, know the songs and the Scripture, and still not recognize the voice of the Lord. We may joke about "growing up born again," but God doesn't have any grandchildren. There needs to be a time in your life when you make a personal choice to accept Christ as Savior and Lord—a moment when *you* decide you will believe God's Word and follow His commands. You do it not because you're expected to do so, but because you have chosen of your own free will to do so and you are born again.

> The LORD called Samuel a third time, and Samuel got up and went to Eli and said, "Here I am; you called me." Then Eli realized that the LORD was calling the boy. So Eli told Samuel, "Go and lie down, and if he calls you, say, 'Speak, LORD, for your servant is listening.'" So Samuel went and lay down in his place. The LORD came and stood there, calling as at the other times, "Samuel! Samuel!" Then Samuel said, "Speak, for your servant is listening" (1 Samuel 3:8-10).

Imagine the fear that must have gripped Samuel's heart as he returned to his bed and waited anxiously. I'm sure his heart leaped when he heard his name called again, and he said with a trembling voice, "Speak, for your servant is listening."

Maybe you responded to God's call at a young age. I can remember being eight years old and knowing that I needed to accept Christ as my Savior and be baptized into Him. It was a terrifying experience for me to walk in front of the entire congregation and speak before two hundred people. I remember trembling for fear when I finally mustered the courage to respond to the invitation. I can still remember the preacher asking me, "Do you believe that Jesus is the Christ?" "Yes," I responded. I came back to church on Sunday night wearing a new pair of white trousers and a white shirt, prepared for baptism. The preacher lowered me into the water and brought me back up, and I felt a tremendous feeling of cleansing and belonging at that moment. I was just a child, but I had made the most important decision of my life.

I've heard that Dwight Moody once returned home from an evangelistic meeting and his wife asked if there were any responses to the invitation. He said, "Yes, there were two-and-a-half conversions." She said, "You mean two adults and a child?" He said, "No, there were two children and one adult." In Dwight Moody's mind, the two children had an entire life to live for God. The adult only had half a life left. It's a tremendous advantage to come to Christ at a young age because you have an entire life to live for Him.

One of the disadvantages to a young conversion is that you might later question the reality of God's call in your life. When you become an adult, you can doubt your experience and wonder if you really have been converted. It was so many years ago and the memory has faded with time that you may question the authenticity of your conversion. Perhaps you drifted away for years and now you're wondering if you still belong, or if God has permanently rejected you because of your gross immorality. Maybe you've gained a great deal of Bible knowledge and an understanding of atonement and grace that you didn't have when you made your first decision to follow Christ, and you wonder if God accepted your limited understanding when you were so young. You might even hear the dramatic testimonies of people who were converted out of a sordid life and think, *That didn't happen to me. I didn't repent with bitter tears. I wonder if I'm saved?*

Don't doubt the reality of God's hand on you as a child. If you responded because other kids were doing so or someone pressured you to do so, then you need to respond to Christ of your own free will. But if you believed in your heart that Jesus was your Savior and you responded out of conviction, then God adopted you into His family. An adopted child is expected to fall, to make mistakes, to want his independence at times, and even to have serious questions and doubts about his bond with his parents. Yet that child belongs to the family unless he chooses to legally withdraw. If you have doubted your relationship with God but know your initial conversion was sincere, then repent of your lack of faith and disobedience, return home like the prodigal son did, and renew the relationship you once had with your heavenly Father. He never left you.

> For he chose us in him before the creation of the world to be holy and blameless in his sight. In love he predestined us to be adopted as his sons through Jesus Christ, in accordance with his pleasure and will—to the praise of his glorious grace, which he has freely given us in the One he loves (Ephesians 1:4-6).

Samuel's Faithful Response

Most people know the story of Samuel saying, "Speak, for your servant is listening," but most of us don't know what God said to Samuel after that.

And the LORD said to Samuel: "See, I am about to do something in Israel that will make the ears of everyone who hears
of it tingle. At that time I will carry out against Eli everything I spoke against his family—from beginning to end. For
I told him that I would judge his family forever because of
the sin he knew about; his sons made themselves con-
temptible, and he failed to restrain them. Therefore, I swore
to the house of Eli, 'The guilt of Eli's house will never be
atoned for by sacrifice or offering'" (1 Samuel 3:11-14).

This was not good news. God was about to bring judgment on
Eli and his sons because of their disregard for the sacred things of
God. Samuel didn't sleep the rest of the night. His mind must have
raced all night. *Did I really hear the voice of the Lord? Can I remember everything that He said? Must I tell Eli or can I keep it to myself?*

Samuel lay down until morning and then opened the doors
of the house of the LORD. He was afraid to tell Eli the vision,
but Eli called him and said, "Samuel, my son." Samuel
answered, "Here I am." "What was it he said to you?" Eli
asked. "Do not hide it from me. May God deal with you, be
it ever so severely, if you hide from me anything he told
you." So Samuel told him everything, hiding nothing from
him. Then Eli said, "He is the LORD; let him do what is good
in his eyes" (1 Samuel 3:15-18).

Nobody likes to share bad news, and Samuel didn't want to tell
Eli what God had said. However, he was faithful to God's call even
though the message was unpleasant.

The Bible says, "Samuel continued as judge over Israel all the
days of his life" (1 Samuel 7:15). A lot of young people grow up
in the church, wander away during their young adult years, and
then return like the prodigal son after they've hit rock bottom. To
his credit, Samuel listened to God as a child and then remained
faithful to the Lord all his life.

Medicine has shifted in recent years from curative to preventive. Instead of only going to the doctor when we're sick, we talk about wellness. We go for regular checkups to avoid serious problems, and we try to eat right, exercise, and take vitamins to stay healthy. The Christian life is preventative, not just curative. The gospel is not just an ambulance at the bottom of the cliff picking up the seriously wounded; it's a fence at the top preventing people from disaster. Jude 24 talks about God as one "who is able to keep you from falling." Harry Emerson Fosdick said, "There is something better than bringing the prodigal son back from the far country—that's keeping him happily in the father's house." Samuel remained faithful to the call he received even though his life was not perfect and he was called upon to endure many disappointments in his ministry. He was disappointed when the people of Israel asked for a king, but he anointed Saul king as God instructed. He was disappointed when Saul drifted away from God and became proud and self-reliant, but Samuel anointed David to be the next king as God instructed. Samuel was probably most disappointed that his own children were not faithful to God.

> When Samuel grew old, he appointed his sons as judges for Israel. The name of his firstborn was Joel and the name of his second was Abijah, and they served at Beersheba. But his sons did not walk in his ways. They turned aside after dishonest gain and accepted bribes and perverted justice (1 Samuel 8:1-3).

It's hard to understand why such good people can sometimes have such rebellious children. Not everyone who grows up in the church remains faithful. Some children have a rebellious nature and nothing the parents do or say can bring them around. Every child has free choice, and some will choose to rebel. Sometimes the parents contribute to their child's rebellion unintentionally: the parents are away from home too much; they're hypocritical,

living a double life that the children see through and resent;
they're too legalistic and rigid, and the children are driven to rebel
to free themselves from all the rules; or they're too passive and the
children get used to living any way they want. Regardless of the
reasons, parents are devastated and spend many sleepless nights
worrying when their children are drifting from God. Parents are
even tempted to blame God and wonder how He could allow
their children to suffer so much and cause so much grief. We don't
know why Samuel's kids didn't follow in his footsteps, but we do
know that Samuel remained faithful to God even though he must
have been severely disappointed.

The Lessons for Us

If you have godly mentors, be grateful

There's a tendency when you move away from home to focus
on the flaws of your parents and your church. You realize as you
get older that things weren't perfect and could have been better.
Remember, no one is perfect. Your parents and mentors probably
did a lot of things right and deserve merit. The Bible says that the
children of godly parents "arise and call [them] blessed" (Proverbs
31:28). If you had parents who took you to church and tried to
raise you to know the Lord, be thankful. They weren't perfect, but
they probably did the best they could. Take them aside some time
and say, "I just want to thank you for introducing me to the Lord.
If it weren't for you, I wouldn't be as wonderful as I am!"

If you encountered God as a child, be respectful

You might be tempted to doubt the reality of your experience,
but God has called and used young people throughout history.
Joseph and Daniel were called by God as teenagers to endure exile
in a foreign land; David was called to fight Goliath when he was
just a shepherd boy; Josiah was only eight years old when he was

crowned king; and Jesus was able to feed five thousand people with the loaves and fish that a little boy brought to Him.

Professional golfer Payne Stewart, who became a Christian two years prior to his tragic death in a plane crash, began his relationship with Christ when his children invited him to go to church with them. Jesus said, "Let the little children come to me, and do not hinder them, for the kingdom of heaven belongs to such as these" (Matthew 19:14).

Paul told Timothy, "Don't let anyone look down on you because you are young" (1 Timothy 4:12). Don't look down on your own youth, either, but believe that God can use the experiences of faith you had as a child to bring honor to Him.

If you grew up "born again," be faithful

If you've been a Christian since the time you were young, you may be tempted to look wistfully over your shoulder at the world and wonder what you've missed. Or you may be tempted to exploit God's grace by ignoring His call, intending to ask forgiveness later. How much better to be able to say with Paul, "I have fought the good fight, I have finished the race, I have kept the faith" (2 Timothy 4:7).

Sin leaves a scar, but faithfulness is a shield against accusation. *Time* magazine named Billy Graham the most influential spiritual man of the century. They said the reason he has been so influential is because there has been no major scandal against his name.[27] Even the world respects the leader who is blameless.

A couple of years ago, I was able to spend some time with my five-year-old grandson during a time when I was struggling with the pressures and temptations of ministry. One night we read Scripture and had prayer before he went to bed, and Charlie prayed for me. He prayed, "Dear God, help Pop to always have the courage to do the right thing." I know he was repeating a prayer he had heard his dad pray for him, but that motivated me to stay the course more than all the encouragement I could have received from spiritual giants I knew. I'm thankful for the godly parents God gave me and the godly mentors I've had along the way, but I'm also thankful for grandchildren whom I don't want to disappoint, who pray, "Help Pop do the right thing."

God uses innocent children to accomplish His will, and He has said that unless we humble ourselves and become like little children, we can't enter the kingdom of heaven. In reality, you don't grow up "born again." You grow up with exposure to spiritual truth, and there comes a time—and sometimes several times—when you must decide on your own to listen to God's call and respond in obedience. When you hear God calling your name, whether you are a child or an adult, don't harden your heart. Have faith, and say with Samuel, "Speak, Lord, for your servant still hears."

8

DAVID:
When Giants Intimidate,

Faith Fights
With Courage

Hebrews 11:32, 34; 1 Samuel 17:1-51

The tallest man to live in modern times was Robert Wadlow from Alton, Illinois. When he was five years old, he was already 5 feet, 6 ½ inches tall. He was over 6 ½ feet tall before he left elementary school. In 1940, when Robert Wadlow died at the age of 32, he was 8 feet, 11.1 inches tall. That's nearly nine feet tall! He weighed 490 pounds (but in his pictures he looks skinny!) and had a shoe size of 37.[28]

Goliath is described in 1 Samuel 17:4 as being "six cubits and a span" (*KJV*). That means Goliath was *over* nine feet tall! He was several inches taller than Robert Wadlow and *two feet* taller than Shaquille O'Neal. Goliath was an enormous man.

Giants That Intimidate Us

Goliath was not just tall; he was a mean-spirited warrior who loved to use his size to intimidate his enemies. He wore a bronze helmet, a two-hundred-pound coat of armor, and bronze leggings. He carried a bronze javelin that was several inches thick and was tipped with a twenty-five-pound iron spearhead! In a day when wars were fought by hand-to-hand combat, he appeared invincible. He stood in the valley and shouted up at the Israelites, "Let's settle this fight right here, one-on-one, me against your best man, winner take all!"

Goliath stood and shouted to the ranks of Israel, "Why do you come out and line up for battle? Am I not a Philistine, and are you not the servants of Saul? Choose a man and have him come down to me. If he is able to fight and kill me, we will become your subjects; but if I overcome him and kill him, you will become our subjects and serve us." Then the Philistine said, "This day I defy the ranks of Israel! Give me a man and let us fight each other" (1 Samuel 17:8-10).

Like a modern-day professional wrestler, Goliath taunted his enemies in an effort to intimidate them. This went on for forty days, twice a day. King Saul was having a problem with morale among his troops. He desperately needed to find someone to fight Goliath because this monster was humiliating Israel.

The Bible tells us that King Saul was one of the largest Israelites—a head taller than his peers (1 Samuel 9:2). He himself was the most likely candidate. Perhaps that's why Goliath called the Israelites "servants of Saul," hoping to remind them who their leader and champion was supposed to be and incite them into pressuring King Saul to fight the battle himself. However, Saul wasn't about to challenge Goliath. He probably rationalized that since he was the king, he was too valuable to risk his own life.

So Saul tried to motivate his soldiers with added incentives: "I will give one of my daughters in marriage to the man who can defeat Goliath!" Saul promised. David would later find out that marrying one of Saul's daughters wasn't much of a reward, but Saul also offered great wealth and a lifetime exemption from taxes. Still, nobody offered to fight Goliath. Instead, "When the Israelites saw the man, they all ran from him in great fear" (1 Samuel 17:24).

You may never meet a nine-foot-tall giant, but we all face giants that can intimidate us. You may be struggling with *giant problems* so huge that you think they're impossible to overcome—indebtedness you can't repay, a disease you can't defeat, an addiction you can't overcome, or a disability you can't face. Or maybe there are *giant people* in your life who are so powerful that they frighten and intimidate you—an intimidating boss who makes you tremble, a cynical professor who mocks God and makes you afraid to share your faith, a domineering mother-in-law who reduces you to tears if she's around you for more than two days, or a rebellious child you can't control. Or maybe your Goliath is a *giant project* that overwhelms you and the challenge is so huge that you can't see yourself tackling it—the degree you're trying to earn, the new job you've been given at work, or the mission trip you promised to take.

On this day in the Valley of Elah, God would raise up a new hero in Israel—a young shepherd boy named David would be the only one courageous enough to fight the intimidating giant. His faith and courage serve as an example to us whenever we face giants that intimidate us.

Unfortunately, David was about to discover a common reality: Whenever you attempt to defeat a giant, there will be people who try to discourage you.

People Who Discourage Us

"David, I want you to take this package to your brothers," his father told him. David gladly obeyed his father's orders. He had three older brothers in the army. A Jewish man wasn't eligible for the army until the age of twenty, so David, who was only in his teens, wasn't old enough to fight for his country. But he was intrigued by the military and welcomed the opportunity to get a glimpse of the action on the front lines. He made his way from his home in Bethlehem toward the Valley of Elah where the Israeli troops were preparing for a big showdown with the hated Philistines.

> Early in the morning David left the flock with a shepherd, loaded up and set out, as Jesse had directed. He reached the camp as the army was going out to its battle positions, shout-

ing the war cry. Israel and the Philistines were drawing up
their lines facing each other (1 Samuel 17:20, 21).

David was captivated by these dramatic events. All the hoopla,
the bragging, the trash talking, and the threats fascinated him.
This wasn't the World Wrestling Federation. It wasn't fake entertainment—this was life and death.

> David left his things with the keeper of supplies, ran to the
> battle lines and greeted his brothers. As he was talking with
> them, Goliath, the Philistine champion from Gath, stepped
> out from his lines and shouted his usual defiance, and David
> heard it (1 Samuel 17:22, 23).

When David brought the sack lunches to his older brothers, he
heard Goliath's taunts. He was furious. He thought, *How dare
anyone speak that way against our God! Why doesn't anyone go and
fight him?*

Then he overheard some Israelite soldiers talking about what
Saul was offering to the man who defeated Goliath, and he said,
"Say that again? Saul will do *what* for the man who defeats
Goliath?" David was beginning to feel the call.

> David asked the men standing near him, "What will be done
> for the man who kills this Philistine and removes this dis-
> grace from Israel? Who is this uncircumcised Philistine that
> he should defy the armies of the living God?" They repeated
> to him what they had been saying and told him, "This is
> what will be done for the man who kills him" (1 Samuel
> 17:26, 27).

People close to you will be cynical

> When Eliab, David's oldest brother, heard him speaking with
> the men, he burned with anger at him and asked, "Why have

you come down here? And with whom did you leave those few sheep in the desert? I know how conceited you are and how wicked your heart is; you came down only to watch the battle" (1 Samuel 17:28).

David's brothers didn't want him nosing around the camp asking questions. Remember that the prophet Samuel was very impressed with Eliab's physical stature (1 Samuel 16:6, 7). Eliab and his brothers probably felt guilty that none of them had the courage to fight Goliath. Then David, the loud-mouthed baby of the family, began asking everybody, "Why doesn't someone do something and shut that stupid giant up?"

Eliab said sarcastically to David, "Why did you really come down here, David, and leave that little flock of sheep you're supposed to be watching? I know what a cocky brat you are—you just wanted to come watch the battle. You don't care who gets hurt here. You think it's all just a big game. Well, it's not a game, David!"

If you entertain the idea of taking on a giant, you will be on the receiving end of critical and derisive remarks, sometimes from the people you thought would have been supportive. They will second-guess your motives, accuse you of being arrogant, and question your sanity. "Do you really think you're capable of accomplishing that? Do you think you're better than everyone else? You just want a little notoriety, that's all. This is just a big ego trip, isn't it?"

Sometimes the most discouraging words come from members of your own family. When Job tried to face with courage his giant of grief and disease, his wife sneered, "Why don't you just curse God and die?" When David entertained the idea of fighting Goliath, his brothers tried to discourage him and send him back to tending the sheep.

But when you're the youngest of eight sons, you develop some tough skin. David wasn't discouraged. Notice how he responded to Eliab's disparaging remarks:

"Now what have I done?" said David. "Can't I even speak?"
He then turned away to someone else and brought up the
same matter, and the men answered him as before (1 Samuel
17:29, 30).

Someone reported to King Saul what David had been saying,
and the king sent for him.

People with more experience than you will be doubtful

When he was brought before the king, David boldly said to
Saul, "Let no one lose heart on account of this Philistine; your
servant will go and fight him" (1 Samuel 17:32). But Saul, too,
discouraged David. Saul replied, "You are not able to go out
against this Philistine and fight him; you are only a boy, and he
has been a fighting man from his youth" (1 Samuel 17:33).

When you attempt to fight a giant, you will have people with
more experience than you give you discouraging counsel. Several
years ago, when our church was trying to get a bank to loan us
millions of dollars for a new building, a bank president cautioned
me: "Bob, do you really think you can get that much money out
of your people without alienating a huge segment of your congregation? People don't like to be hounded for money, and you're
moving seven miles away. Don't you think you'll lose a large percentage of your membership?"

I knew that if God blessed us, we wouldn't have to "hound"
people for money, and God has been faithful. I was reminded that
experienced people can discourage you from challenging a giant.
They'll say things like, "If you go to the mission field, you'll miss
your family and you won't be able to adapt. It's too dangerous."
"You're not going to change that professor. He'll make a fool out
of you. Don't speak up or you'll get yourself in trouble." "Don't
take that promotion. It's too much pressure."

That's why it is so important that we get counsel from people who are in touch with God's will, who will give us wise advice, and who will believe in God's ability to use us. David later wrote, "Blessed is the man who does not walk in the counsel of the wicked or stand in the way of sinners or sit in the seat of mockers. But his delight is in the law of the LORD, and on his law he meditates day and night" (Psalm 1:1, 2). David was so in touch with God that the king didn't discourage him.

> But David said to Saul, "Your servant has been keeping his father's sheep. When a lion or a bear came and carried off a sheep from the flock, I went after it, struck it and rescued the sheep from its mouth. When it turned on me, I seized it by its hair, struck it and killed it. Your servant has killed both the lion and the bear; this uncircumcised Philistine will be like one of them, because he has defied the armies of the living God. The LORD who delivered me from the paw of the lion and the paw of the bear will deliver me from the hand of this Philistine." Saul said to David, "Go, and the LORD be with you" (1 Samuel 17:34-37).

Remember that sometime earlier the prophet Samuel had secretly anointed David to be King Saul's successor, and the Bible says that the Spirit of the Lord came upon David at that time (1 Samuel 16:13). David was fearless in battle because he had experienced the Lord's empowerment before in frightening situations. His victories in obscurity had prepared him for success in the public arena. David said, "I can do this because the Lord has been with me before and he will be with me again." Saul finally acquiesced and said, "O.K., David. You go—and may the Lord be with you."

People who care about you will try to be helpful

Saul, the pragmatist, then tried to help David by offering his own armor. Saul knew he wasn't going to need it any time soon!

> Then Saul dressed David in his own tunic. He put a coat of
> armor on him and a bronze helmet on his head. David fas-
> tened on his sword over the tunic and tried walking around,
> because he was not used to them. "I cannot go in these," he
> said to Saul, "because I am not used to them." So he took
> them off (1 Samuel 17:38, 39).

Have you ever watched a peewee football practice when the
kids put on their equipment for the first time? Those little guys go
waddling all over the football field with their shoulder pads shift-
ing to one side and helmets falling down over their eyes. They can
barely move.

I picture Saul as a six-foot-six-inch-tall adult, size 52 long, trying to put his armor on David who is five-feet-nine and a size 40
regular (the perfect size for spiritual people!). The armor doesn't
fit. "I can't move!" David said, and he took the armor off.

When you face a giant, there will be well-meaning people who
will say to you, "If you're going to take on this giant, you need my
worldly expertise. You need to fight worldly giants with worldly
weapons or you'll be eaten alive." Pragmatic people will say to you,
"You've got to bribe the politicians and use some leverage. That's
the way the game is played." "Don't try to pay back that debt. Just
file for bankruptcy." "Accept the fact that the marriage is over, file
for divorce, and get all the money you can out of him." "Go ahead
and sue. You have the legal right to pain and suffering. Everybody
does it."

But the Bible says, "For though we live in the world, we do not
wage war as the world does. The weapons we fight with are not
the weapons of the world. On the contrary, they have divine
power to demolish strongholds" (2 Corinthians 10:3, 4). David
knew he didn't need Saul's equipment or encouragement; he just
needed God's empowerment.

The God Who Empowers Us

In order to defeat a giant bigger than ourselves, we must tap into a source of power larger than the giant. Overcoming the Goliaths in your life requires putting your faith in the God who is larger than any giant, who can empower you and give you the victory. With God on your side, the giant can be defeated. David's example gives us several practical instructions we can follow to ensure that our faith is in the God who empowers us and that the giant is defeated with God's help.

Make sure you have the right motives

David asked twice about the reward that had been offered to the one who defeated Goliath, so David's motives weren't totally service-oriented. He was also interested in the money and the pretty girl. But David's primary concern was that the name of God was being blasphemed. "Who is this uncircumsized Philistine," he kept asking, "that he should defy the armies of the living God?" (1 Samuel 17:26).

If you want proof of David's unselfish motives, turn to the book of Psalms and read what he writes about his battle with Goliath. There are 150 psalms, and not once does David even mention his victory over the Philistine giant! If I had been David, I'd have worked the story into the songs once in a while (like maybe every other psalm)! I'd have introduced most of my songs by saying, "That reminds me of a battle I once had with a giant." But not so with David. He fought the battle for the glory of God, not his own ego.

The first step you should take before challenging a giant is to examine your motives. David told his son Solomon, "And you, my son Solomon, acknowledge the God of your father, and serve him with wholehearted devotion and with a willing mind, for the LORD searches every heart and understands every motive behind the thoughts. If you seek him, he will be found by you; but if you forsake him, he will reject you forever" (1 Chronicles 28:9).

Why are you taking on this giant? Do you want fame, fortune, power, or ego gratification, or is your motive to honor God, provide for your family, or help others? God is going to bless those who check their egos at the door. Paul wrote, "Do nothing out of selfish ambition or vain conceit, but in humility consider others better than yourselves. Each of you should look not only to your own interests, but also to the interests of others" (Philippians 2:3, 4).

Put your confidence in God, not yourself

When Saul asked, "How can a kid like you fight a man like him?" David insisted, "The Lord who saved me from the claws and teeth of the lion and the bear will save me from this Philistine!" David had a holy boldness because he was confident in the Lord. He didn't just have faith in himself—he had faith in God. He would later write, "My help comes from the LORD, the Maker of heaven and earth" (Psalm 121:2). In the New Testament we're reminded, "This is the victory that has overcome the world, even our faith" (1 John 5:4).

Sir Laurence Olivier said that to be a good actor one needs to be "humble enough to prepare and confident enough to perform." David had both humility and confidence—a rare, valuable combination. While everyone else was saying, "He's so big, how can we beat him?" David was saying, "He's so big, how can I miss?"

Whenever we face intimidating giants, we often lack confidence because we haven't developed what athletes call "positive memory." If a golfer stands over a three-foot putt and remembers the last time he missed a putt that close, he's much more likely to miss it again. But if he has developed a positive memory, he recalls how he hit ten in a row from the same distance on the practice green. He says to himself, "I'm good at this distance," and he's likely to make the putt.

We recall defeats and failures much more quickly than victories and accomplishments. Instead, like a good athlete, we need to develop a positive memory, recalling times past when God has given us victory. David had confidence in God because he remembered God's victories in his life. The Bible instructs us, "Finally, brothers, whatever is true, whatever is noble, whatever is right, whatever is pure, whatever is lovely, whatever is admirable—if anything is excellent or praiseworthy—think about such things" (Philippians 4:8). And just a few verses later we're reminded, "I can do everything through him who gives me strength" (Philippians 4:13).

Stay with your strengths

> Then he took his staff in his hand, chose five smooth stones from the stream, put them in the pouch of his shepherd's bag and, with his sling in his hand, approached the Philistine (1 Samuel 17:40).

David was good with a slingshot, having practiced by the hour while he was watching his sheep. He could whirl that sling around his head, release the stone, and knock a chip off a stump fifty yards away. When it came time to fight Goliath, David decided not to use Saul's spear or a bow from one of his brothers. He decided to stay with his strength even though the slingshot looked funny to Goliath.

I've known preachers who normally preach from a brief outline change their style when they're asked to speak at a large national convention. They'll type out a manuscript and woodenly, nervously read it at the convention, thinking they're going to sound more intelligent or better prepared. People walk away saying, "I've heard him do better at his home church. I wonder what happened."

Maybe you've seen a basketball coach head into a big game against a giant opponent and get so nervous that he changes his lineup to counter the opposing team's strengths. Usually, the team continuity is disrupted and the team doesn't play as well as it normally would have had the coach stayed with the approach that had got him there.

Have you ever seen a young man who is so intimidated by a pretty girl that his whole personality changes when he's around her? He tries to be funny or athletic or clever, and he's not. The girl isn't impressed because he comes across as inauthentic. He would have made a better impression if he had just been himself. A giant-killer doesn't try to be someone he's not.

Verbally give honor to God

When David appeared before Goliath, the giant snarled, "Am I a dog, that you come at me with sticks?" The Scripture says "the Philistine cursed David by his gods" and said, "Come here, . . . and I'll give your flesh to the birds of the air and the beasts of the field!" (1 Samuel 17:43, 44). But David didn't respond with trash talking of his own. Instead, he boasted about the power of God. Notice how many times in this next passage that David gives honor to the Lord Almighty, the God of Israel:

> David said to the Philistine, "You come against me with sword and spear and javelin, but I come against you in *the name of the LORD Almighty, the God of the armies of Israel,* whom you have defied. This day *the LORD* will hand you over to me, and I'll strike you down and cut off your head. Today I will give the carcasses of the Philistine army to the birds of the air and the beasts of the earth, and the whole world will know that there is a *God in Israel*. All those gathered here will know that it is not by sword or spear that *the LORD* saves; for the battle is *the LORD's*, and *he* will give all of you into our hands" (1 Samuel 17:45-47, emphasis mine).

When a giant tries to intimidate you, give glory to God. When your professor ridicules you for believing in creation and you know you don't have all the right answers, you can still say, "You're right, professor. I do believe the Bible. I believe it is God's Word from cover to cover."

When your doctor tells you that your condition is inoperable and you should accept the inevitable, you can tell him, "Doctor, I believe there's a God in heaven who answers prayers, and I'm going to put my trust in Him."

When your adversary Satan, the most intimidating giant, scoffs, "You don't really believe in life after death, do you?" You can say, "Get behind me, Satan. The God who raised Jesus from the dead two thousand years ago is able to raise me also."

David said, "Let the redeemed of the LORD say so" (Psalm 107:2, *KJV*). There is tremendous power released when we verbalize our faith in God.

Several months ago, I was honored to be asked to preach the funeral service for baseball legend Pee Wee Reese. Before the funeral, the director introduced me to the honorary pallbearers: Sandy Koufax, Duke Snider, Clyde King, Carl Erskine, and some others. Those guys were major league heroes when I was growing up. They were bigger than life! Now they were sitting in front of me as I preached.

A friend asked me, "Doesn't that make you nervous to speak in front of those players and reporters?" Yes, of course it does. My favorite definition of courage is this: "Courage is not the absence of fear, but action in spite of fear." It's not wrong to be afraid. Courage is being afraid and doing it anyway.

Two things struck me as I met those guys. First, they were aging men facing the giant of death just like the rest of us. Second, they needed Christ. I needed to stay with what I normally did at funerals and exalt Jesus Christ. After talking about the life of Pee Wee Reese, I said in the final moments of the message,

> I want you to know that I believe with all my heart that there is life after death. I don't believe it because it's wishful think-

ing at a funeral. I believe it because Jesus Christ died, was buried, and conquered the grave. I believe His Word is true: "I am the resurrection and the life. He who believes in me will live, even though he dies."

I didn't say anything new or profound, but I think there is power in just affirming the truth. I may not have slain any giants that day, but one of those players, a strong Christian, did thank me for unashamedly sharing the gospel. "Several of these guys really needed to hear that," he said.

Hebrews 10:23 says, "Let us hold unswervingly to the hope we profess, for he who promised is faithful." David said confidently, "I come against you in the name of the Lord. The battle is the Lord's and he will give you into our hands."

Move toward the giant

"As the Philistine moved closer to attack him, David ran quickly toward the battle line to meet him" (1 Samuel 17:48). We're tempted to run away and hide from the giants in our lives, or to stalk them, looking forever for a point of vulnerability. Most often the best response is not to run, but to attack quickly.

An old philosopher said, "If you have to swallow a frog, don't look at it very long!" If there's some unpleasantry in your life, get it over with. Don't stand around analyzing it forever; confront it as soon as possible. Usually the longer you wait, the more intimidating the giant appears and the more fear you accumulate. If you have an unpleasant phone call to make, pick up the phone and call as soon as possible. If you have a difficult paper to write, begin attacking it early in the semester. If you have a Christian friend who has strayed from the faith and you know you should contact him, don't keep putting it off—do it today. You will feel so much better about yourself when you run toward the battle line than when you run away, hide, and make excuses for your delays.

Finish the job

David completed the task. "Reaching into his bag and taking out a stone, he slung it and struck the Philistine on the forehead. The stone sank into his forehead, and he fell facedown on the ground" (1 Samuel 17:49).

In spite of his armor, Goliath had one vulnerable spot. As Goliath drew his sword and lumbered toward him, David quickly ran toward the giant with his slingshot whirling overhead. A pitcher can throw a baseball nearly one hundred miles per hour. A slingshot in the hands of an expert could probably fire a stone even faster than that. David's hours of practice had prepared him for this moment. When he was just a few feet away from the giant, he let the stone fly and it hit Goliath right in his most vulnerable spot—his forehead—and he was knocked unconscious.

We usually end the story right there, but the next two verses relate how David finished the job:

> So David triumphed over the Philistine with a sling and a stone; without a sword in his hand he struck down the Philistine and killed him. David ran and stood over him. He took hold of the Philistine's sword and drew it from the scabbard. After he killed him, he cut off his head with the sword. When the Philistines saw that their hero was dead, they turned and ran (1 Samuel 17:50, 51).

David had a killer instinct. He didn't quit until the job was finished. Goliath would not live to intimidate, blaspheme, or fight again, and David was an instant hero.

It takes courage to face a giant, but it takes perseverance to finish the task. If you're challenging indebtedness, don't quit until the last bill is paid and you're no longer paying interest every month. If you're pursuing a degree, stay with it until you receive your diploma. If you're determined to conquer an addiction, don't quit just because you've proved you can walk straight for six months. Follow through and stay sober.

Ross Brodfuehrer wrote, "The hiss of fear or the whisper of faith—which voice dominates you? God may not outshout Satan, but He will outperform him. Put your trust in him."[29] Remember that courage isn't the absence of fear, but action in spite of fear. David sang,

> The LORD is my light and my salvation—whom shall I fear? The LORD is the stronghold of my life—of whom shall I be afraid? When evil men advance against me to devour my flesh, when my enemies and my foes attack me, they will stumble and fall. Though an army besiege me, my heart will not fear; though war break out against me, even then will I be confident. One thing I ask of the LORD, this is what I seek: that I may dwell in the house of the LORD all the days of my life (Psalm 27:1-4a).

Linda Surbeck, a Christian woman from our church, courageously took on a giant because of her commitment to Christ. A few years ago, Linda was nominated for two awards in the international organization of which she is a member. That particular year, the annual meeting was held in Washington, D.C., and the local chapter was responsible for the opening day entertainment. To the embarrassment of Linda and several others, the group sponsored a short dance production that glorified homosexuality. Linda said the skit was not only embarrassing, but also extraordinarily offensive.

The awards were to be given out the next evening, and that night Linda faced a giant. She was angered and hurt by what had happened, and she wrestled over what to do. The next morning, she informed the president of the association that she would not be party to such an antibiblical display. She was considering withdrawing her membership from an organization that allowed such a blatantly immoral demonstration. She decided she would not be present at the awards ceremony and handed the president a written statement to be read on her behalf if she was asked to accept an award.

Her action immediately caused a great deal of discussion among the leaders of the organization. At the awards dinner that night, the entire Washington chapter went on stage and apologized for the previous evening's production. They promised that future productions would be in good taste. The giant was defeated! Linda is completely convinced that the Lord was using her, and she is glad to have had the opportunity to take a stand for Jesus Christ.

Linda learned that God can use one person to defeat a giant if you're willing to put your faith in Christ and take a courageous stand.

9

ELIJAH:
When Life Caves In,
Faith Hopes

Hebrews 11:35; 1 Kings 17:8-24

Chad and Heidi Whitaker were still newlyweds when they first heard the doctor say the word "leukemia." They had been married for six months when Heidi, a beautiful, athletic twenty-four-year-old, began having some health problems. The doctor sat down with Chad and Heidi in his office and delivered the bad news. "Heidi, you have leukemia," he said.

How do you react when life caves in?

The doctor says it's leukemia, your mate says she doesn't love you anymore, your parents announce they're getting a divorce, your daughter says she's pregnant, the telephone rings and your mother says your father has passed away. . . . There must be a thousand tragedies that can knock the props right out from under you. When it happens, there is a sickening feeling in your stomach and it seems like life is falling apart. How do you react? Do you throw a temper tantrum? Make jokes? Withdraw? Get angry with God? Rejoice?

How you react in the moment of crisis reveals much more about your faith than months of ordinary living. Years ago, I watched a mechanic fix a slowly-leaking inner tube by attaching an air hose to it and blowing it up larger than its normal size. With the additional pressure inside, he could hear the hissing of air through the weak point of the tube and knew which spot needed to be repaired. God allows pressure to come into our lives so that we can identify our weak points and begin to correct them.

Such was the case with Elijah when he was at the home of the widow of Zarephath. God was preparing Elijah to be His spokesman in the midst of a tense and evil world. Elijah had already confronted King Ahab and announced that there would be a severe drought in Israel because the people were worshiping the false god Baal instead of Jehovah. As a prophet of doom, Elijah was not popular with Ahab, so after his bad news, Elijah fled. He became a fugitive, hiding out in the Kerith Ravine. He drank from the river and ate the food delivered by ravens sent by God (1 Kings 17:1-6).

When the brook dried up, God humbled Elijah further by sending him to an impoverished widow at Zarephath who would take care of him. For a while, everything went well. In the midst of a severe drought they had plenty to eat because every day God miraculously refilled the widow's vessel of oil and replenished her barrel of flour (1 Kings 17:7-16).

This widow at Zarephath, living in the heart of Baal worship, was impressed with Elijah's God and was thankful for Elijah's presence. Then one day life suddenly caved in for both of them.

A Child's Death

Tragedy struck the widow's home when her only son became ill and died. The Scripture reads, "Some time later the son of the woman who owned the house became ill. He grew worse and worse, and finally stopped breathing" (1 Kings 17:17).

I've witnessed a lot of tragedy in my ministry and performed hundreds of funerals. I don't know if there is anything more tragic than the death of a child. The two-year-old child of a young couple in our church drowned in a swimming pool a few months ago. That horrible night friends and relatives gathered at the home to try to comfort the family, but there was nothing that could be done to mend the mother's broken heart. The coroner pulled me aside and said, "Bob, I've been around death a lot, and there's something different about a mother's cry when she has just lost one of her babies. It comes from the soul." I agree. There is something deep in a mother's soul that weeps when her child passes away prematurely.

After I performed the funeral service for a seven-year-old boy who had died of leukemia, his mother approached me and said, "Bob, if words could have helped, you would have helped today." There is nothing that can be said to ease a mother's pain under such circumstances.

There are several reasons why the death of a child is such a difficult experience.

It is unexpected

An older woman in her eighties sobbed when we informed her of her daughter's death. Her daughter was in her mid-sixties, but the mother said, "You just never think your child will die before you. You always think you'll go first." No matter what the child's age, parents assume they will precede the child in death.

It is unfair

When a young child so full of life and potential dies, it upsets our instinctive sense of justice. It only seems fair that every person be permitted to live "three score years and ten." That child will never know what it's like to drive a car, graduate from high school, get married, and have children. It seems unfair. We're tempted to question God's justice. If we were in charge of the universe, bad people would die at eighty and good people would die at one hundred, but nobody would die young. Everyone would have a fair chance.

It is uncertain

Parents feel responsible for teaching and preparing their children for what will happen to them in the future. But how can we prepare them for a mysterious journey we've not taken?

The son of the Zarephath widow didn't die suddenly—he became increasingly ill. He must have asked his mother, "Am I going to die? What's dying like?" It must have been difficult for her to answer.

What is it like to die? What should a mother tell her child under such circumstances? Is death like Shirley MacLaine's out-of-body experiences where the spirit just floats pleasantly toward the moon? Is death a greeting from a sinister grim reaper? Is it a cold river to be crossed?

Hebrews 2:15 says that Christ came to "free those who all their lives were held in slavery by their fear of death." Some people are so petrified of the mystery of death that they are slaves to fear. They think about death constantly or else try to avoid the subject altogether. Christ came to set us free from the fear of death. Some fear of death is natural. God gives us an instinct for self-preservation that remains strong so that we aren't careless. But He wants to free us from phobias about dying so we can live abundantly every day and accept death gracefully when it comes.

Christ died on the cross for our sins and then rose from the dead to show that we can do it too. Though I have never gone through the death experience, I have a Savior who has, and He assures me that He will be with me through the process and that I need not be afraid. I can say to my children, "The words of David are true—'Yea, though I walk through the valley of the shadow of death, I will fear no evil: for thou art with me'" (Psalm 23:4, *KJV*).

At many of the funeral services I've preached, I've relayed a story that an old preacher told, comparing the death experience to that of a little boy who took a trip with his father:

> The father and son were headed to the market when they came to a raging river. The bridge had been washed out, and all that was left were the pylons jutting up out of the water. His father gripped the boy's hand and helped him step across the river on the pylons. At times the boy was suspended just

inches above the raging current, held only by the grip of his father around his wrist.

They stayed too long at the market that day, and at dusk they started back home. As they traveled, the father heard his boy whimpering and asked him what was wrong. The boy sobbed, "Daddy, we barely made it across the river in the light! How will we ever make it across in the dark?"

The father picked up his son and began to carry him home. Soon the tired boy fell asleep. When he awakened the next morning, he was in his own room, the light was beaming through the window, and he could see his father standing in the doorway smiling.

That's what the death experience is like. That which we fear the most, we never experience. We go to sleep in the Father's arms and awaken in the Father's house.

A Mother's Bitterness

When her child died, such words of comfort meant little to the Zarephath widow. She was left alone to grieve the loss of her son, and she was bitter. "She said to Elijah, 'What do you have against me, man of God? Did you come to remind me of my sin and kill my son?'" (1 Kings 17:18).

Understanding her bitterness

Those who have studied the grief process report that we go through various stages of grief, usually in the same order: shock, denial, anger, depression, and acceptance. The length of the stages depends on the severity of the loss and the temperament of the individual. When the tragedy is especially severe, it can take a person as long as two years, or even longer, to complete all five stages of grief. Perhaps since her son had been sick and she was prepared for his death, the Zarephath woman jumped right to the anger stage. When her son died, she was immediately embittered. She blamed God—and Elijah who represented him—for her pain.

It may be easy to understand this woman's bitterness. Her faith in Elijah's God was just blossoming. Jehovah had spoken to her and instructed her to feed Elijah, and she had witnessed the miraculous daily replenishing of the oil and flour. Then, just about the time she was gaining confidence in Jehovah, her life caved in. What kind of cruel, deceptive God would reward obedience with death? If He was really taking care of her daily needs, how could He let this happen? She was a widow, so she was already acquainted with grief. How much more pain would God call her to bear?

Dispelling her misconception

Did you notice that the woman connected her tragedy with her sin? Look again at 1 Kings 17:18. She said to Elijah, "What do you have against me, man of God? Did you come to *remind me of my sin* and kill my son?" The Zarephath widow concluded that the death of her son was a direct punishment for her sins, and the presence of this righteous man of God only made her mistakes even more glaring.

People commonly mistake tragedy as God's direct judgment for a person's sins. If you suffer, it must be because God is displeased with you and is punishing you. This woman in Zarephath believed that. So did the friends of Job. So did the disciples of Jesus. The Gospel of John tells of a time when Jesus and His disciples encountered a man along the road who had been born blind. His disciples asked him, "Rabbi, who sinned, this man or his parents, that he was born blind?"

"Neither this man nor his parents sinned," said Jesus, "but this happened so that the work of God might be displayed in his life" (John 9:2, 3).

Most pain is not directly connected to our sin. There are some exceptions: If you drink too much, you can get liver disease; if you have sex outside of marriage, you risk contracting a venereal disease; if you steal, you may have to spend time in jail. But those exceptions are obvious—the consequences are directly related to our actions. A false teaching that remains popular to this day says that if you are suffering, it must be because you don't have enough faith in God to help you or there is some unconfessed sin in your life.

That simply is not true according to Scripture. Jesus told His followers, "In this world you will have trouble" (John 16:33). We live in a world that is contaminated by sin and each of us will experience some of the fallout. The death of the widow's son had nothing to do with her own sin, but had everything to do with the fact that he lived in a world contaminated with germs and viruses and diseases.

Steve Brown says that he believes every time a pagan contracts cancer, a Christian gets cancer too, so that the world can see the difference in how the two people handle their adversity; every time a pagan goes bankrupt, a Christian goes bankrupt too, so the world can witness the difference in their reactions. Whether or not God is making sure tragedies are equally distributed, Scripture is clear that Christians are not exempt from the random troubles of this world.

A man I know had a terminal disease and was told by a relative that if he had enough faith in God and confessed his sins, he would get well because God wants us wealthy and happy. That family prayed and claimed healing, but it was not realistic. The man died. I was so angry at the false teaching that had caused so much confusion and tension that I wrote a seven-minute diatribe in my next sermon, explaining why we shouldn't believe that obedience always brings immediate blessings or that disobedience always brings punishment. I reduced that seven-minute segment to one sentence: Jesus was poor and Paul was sick. What more should I have to say?

When tragedies occur in your life, don't ask, "Where have I sinned? What have I done to deserve this?" Jesus said you will have trouble in this world. Even good people will experience calamity. Even the righteous are not immune. Christ never promised that if you follow Him, you would be free from suffering. In fact, He promised just the opposite.

A Prophet's Faith

In contrast to the woman's bitter reaction, the prophet Elijah maintained his faith in God. Elijah not only believed that God could carry them through the tragedy and could bring good from evil, he even believed that God had the power to raise the boy back to life. In the midst of this trial, Elijah exhibited some characteristics that are worth emulating whenever we face troubles of our own.

He stayed calm

When the widow spewed her bitter words at Elijah, he didn't scream back. He didn't try to refute her bad theology with arguments she wasn't ready to hear. And he didn't panic and start shouting at God. He calmly said, "Give me your son."

When tragedy strikes or the pressure is upon us, we can testify to our faith in God by maintaining our poise. Jesus was always calm under pressure. He got angry on a couple of occasions, like when He cleansed the temple, but even then His anger was under control. He never panicked even when His life was in jeopardy. When Pilate was wringing his hands, Caiaphas was ripping his garment, and the disciples were running for fear, Jesus remained calm. Everyone was in awe of His strength in the midst of His trial. Elijah did his best to maintain that same kind of poise.

The Bible says that one of the fruits of the spirit is self-control (Galatians 5:23). When you lose control—when you shout, hit, weep uncontrollably, go into a trance, or have an anxiety attack— you are not bringing glory to God. When you can keep calm in the midst of a storm, you honor Christ.

There's an anonymous story about an old Chinese man who had a young son and one horse. One day when the boy was riding the horse, the gate was left open and the horse wandered off. The child and the horse were lost. The neighbors came to the man to convey their condolences, saying, "We're sorry that you have nothing left. That's so bad." The father replied, "How do you know it's bad?"

Several days later, the boy and the horse returned, leading thirteen wild horses back to the corral. The neighbors came to congratulate the old man, saying, "How wonderful that you now have fourteen horses and your son is back home!"

"How do you know it's good?" the old man asked.

A few days later, the boy was trying to ride one of those wild horses when he fell off and broke his leg. The neighbors said to the old man, "We're so sorry that your son has broken his leg. That's so bad."

"How do you know it's bad?" the old man replied.

The next day, a tyrannical warlord came through, picking up all able-bodied young men to fight his battles. All the young men in the town were taken except the boy with the broken leg.

That story could go on forever! The point is that we have such a limited perspective, we don't know what circumstances in life are good or bad. We can only trust that God's promise is true: ". . . in all things God works for the good of those who love him, who have been called according to his purpose" (Romans 8:28). I'm not suggesting that we have a stoical attitude toward life and never hurt or weep, but if we believe Romans 8:28 is true, then we can keep calm in the midst of tragedy.

He sought privacy

Elijah took the dead boy from his mother's arms and carried him to the upper room where Elijah had been staying (1 Kings 17:19). He was going to pray for a miracle, but he was determined to do it in private. Years later, Jesus gave us this advice about prayer:

> And when you pray, do not be like the hypocrites, for they love to pray standing in the synagogues and on the street corners to be seen by men. I tell you the truth, they have received their reward in full. But when you pray, go into your room, close the door and pray to your Father, who is unseen. Then your Father, who sees what is done in secret, will reward you (Matthew 6:5, 6).

Some things are so sacred that they're not to be done in a crowd. Jesus would often take a person aside to perform a healing, then say to the one healed, "Don't tell anyone about this." When Jesus raised Jairus's daughter from the dead, He went inside, dismissed the professional mourners, and went up into the bedroom of the girl with only Peter, James, John, and the girl's parents. Jesus took the girl by the hand and said, "Talitha koum!" (which means, "Little girl, I say to you, get up!"), and the girl got up (Mark 5:41, 42). It was such an intimate moment that Jesus didn't want it ruined by a big crowd. He wasn't performing the miracle for show.

What a contrast to many modern-day faith healers who announce their intent to heal, call attention to their deeds, and invite people to come and see. Jesus didn't exploit people or call attention to himself, and neither did the prophet Elijah.

Don't be too quick to broadcast your great deeds in advance. Just do them quietly and allow God to get the credit. Don't parade your piety or power in front of people. When life caves in, don't immediately brag to others, "I know I'll be strong." Instead, go through the crisis with God's help. Later, when people ask you how you survived your trial, you can give the glory to God.

He prayed

> Then [Elijah] cried out to the LORD, "O LORD my God, have you brought tragedy also upon this widow I am staying with,

by causing her son to die?" Then he stretched himself out on
the boy three times and cried to the LORD, "O LORD my
God, let this boy's life return to him!" (1 Kings 17:20, 21).

Notice some characteristics of Elijah's prayer of faith.

It was an honest prayer. Elijah himself didn't understand why
the boy was allowed to die, and he expressed his doubts to God.
"Why have you brought this tragedy?" he asked. One of the reasons Elijah wanted to be alone was so he could articulate his feelings to God. He kept calm in front of the woman, but in private
he expressed his honest questions to God. The famous German
philosopher Johann Wolfgang Goethe used to say, "Tell me your
faith. I have doubts enough of my own." There is a time and place
to express your doubts. When Elijah was alone, he was honest
with God.

A preacher whose young son had just died stood quietly near
the casket as visitors filed by to give their condolences. He thought
he would scream when people kept saying, "This was God's will,"
and "The Lord will see you through." Even though he was the
preacher of the church, all the usual spiritual-sounding clichés
seemed so trite in his moment of grief. Finally he dismissed himself, got into his car, and started driving. He got on the interstate
and began screaming at God, pounding on the steering wheel. He
even cursed. He just didn't understand how God could permit this
to happen to him. When he was finished with his tirade, he felt
the presence of God. He was reminded that God could handle it
all, even his anger. And he knew that with God's help, he could
handle it as well. He returned to the funeral home to finish the
night of visitation and to give testimony of his faith in God.

It was a persistent prayer. Three times Elijah cried out to the
Lord (1 Kings 17:21). The Bible tells us not to give up in prayer
(Luke 18:1-8; 1 Thessalonians 5:17). God wants us to keep on
asking, keep on seeking, and keep on knocking. When we are
forced to pray persistently, our priorities become more properly

arranged. Elijah didn't quit praying when his initial prayer wasn't answered.

It was a prayer of faith. Elijah prayed that God would raise the boy back to life. Up to that point in history, there was no account of anyone ever being revived after death. Elijah was asking for something that had never happened before! He had never seen anyone come back to life, but he believed God could do the impossible. The God who had stopped the rain, fed him by ravens, and replenished the widow's flour and oil could raise the dead.

God wants us to pray for big things. I love the poem that says,

> Thou art coming to a king!
> Large petitions with thee bring!
> For His strength and power are such,
> Thou canst never ask too much!

God is not some kind of genie whose will can be manipulated by our wishes. He is a loving Father who is complimented when His children come to Him with bold requests.

He worked

Elijah made every effort to answer the prayer on his own. He carried the boy upstairs. That takes effort! He stretched himself out on the boy three times and cried out to God for the boy's life. Jewish law forbade the touching of a dead body, but Elijah's compassion overcame him. He didn't know what else to do and he was determined to do something.

Some commentators have suggested that Elijah performed mouth-to-mouth resuscitation on the boy. Others say that the warmth of Elijah's body generated a heartbeat in the boy. Yet Elijah didn't raise the boy back to life by his own efforts—God performed a miracle. However, Elijah was making every effort to bring an answer to his prayer.

The old slogan is true: We should pray as if everything depends on God and work as if everything depends on us. You can't just pray that God will bless your children; you must also discipline them, teach them, and set a proper example. You can't just pray that God will provide your church with growth and a positive testimony; you must be willing to sacrifice hours of time and effort to make it happen. You can't just pray that God will make you healthy; you must eat right, exercise, and give your body proper rest.

Will Rogers pointed out that almost every time you see a picture of a pilgrim praying, there is a gun by his side. The pilgrim was going to do his part to see that the prayer was answered. If he was praying for a meal, he was going to hunt for an answer. If he was praying for protection, he stood ready to defend himself.

Some people say, "God helps those who help themselves." That may not always be true, but your labor shows the seriousness of your prayer and makes it more likely that your desire will be met.

In any situation, you can't know whether God will choose to intervene by His miraculous hand or whether He expects you to learn certain lessons and accomplish certain things by your own efforts. Elijah wanted to make sure God knew how serious he was, and he was willing to do anything it took to see that his prayer was answered.

He gave God the glory

The LORD heard Elijah's cry, and the boy's life returned to him, and he lived. Elijah picked up the child and carried him down from the room into the house. He gave him to his mother and said, "Look, your son is alive!" Then the woman said to Elijah, "Now I know that you are a man of God and that the word of the LORD from your mouth is the truth" (1 Kings 17:22-24).

When the woman received back her son, she didn't praise Elijah's medical abilities. She praised his God. There was something about Elijah's character and conduct that brought honor to God and not to himself.

Jesus said, "Let your light shine before men, that they may see your good deeds and praise your Father in heaven" (Matthew 5:16). When God works through you to teach, heal, comfort, or inspire, don't take the honor yourself. Find some way to give glory to God.

I heard Steve Brown tell of meeting a woman who expressed gratitude to him for his tape and radio ministry. She said, "Before I began listening to you, I didn't know Christ. Now I do. I just love hearing you preach. I want you to meet a friend of mine." She grabbed her friend's arm, looked at Steve, and said, "Tell me your name again." The fact that the woman had forgotten Steve's name was a compliment to his efforts to give glory to God and not himself. It didn't matter to Steve that the woman didn't know his name. What mattered was that she knew the name of Jesus.

The lessons we learn from Elijah can be summarized in one sentence: When life caves in, don't panic; have faith in God and do what you can. Notice that I said, "*When* life caves in," not "*if* life caves in." Into every life a little rain must fall. And some lives even experience repeated bolts of lightning! Remember that the tragedy you are suffering is not a sign of personal sin, but evidence that you live in a fallen world.

Don't panic. Don't blame God and become an angry, resentful person. Don't let it make you bitter; let it make you better. Trust that God's Word is true: All things work together for the good of those who love Him. Wait on God's perfect timing.

But also work. Don't sit back with your arms folded and do nothing. In case God chooses to use your efforts to His glory, make sure you're doing what you can.

For four years, Heidi Whitaker battled leukemia, with her husband Chad faithfully by her side. Three rounds of chemotherapy caused every strand of her long brown hair to fall out. She spent months in the hospital.

The doctors said her only hope was to undergo a risky and painful bone marrow transplant. Chad and Heidi prayed that God would take away the leukemia, but they also decided to do all they could to help heal her. They planned to go to Seattle for the transplant and, in the meantime, they waited for a donor.

A match was finally found, and Chad and Heidi prepared to leave. We prayed for them and sent them off, expecting them to return in about one hundred days. Chad sent us e-mails almost every day telling of Heidi's progress. "Heidi had a good day today. She was able to take five laps around the hospital hallway," he would write. Or, "Heidi is in a lot of pain today. Please pray for us." Or, "Heidi got off the respirator today! Praise God, and keep praying!"

But Heidi got a severe case of graft-versus-host disease. Her body was rejecting the new bone marrow. Seven months later, Chad continued to send e-mails from Seattle asking us to pray for Heidi's recovery. The drugs that were given to Heidi to help her overcome the GVHD caused her bones to deteriorate, and at one point she suffered from fourteen stress fractures in her back. Every movement was painful. Even in the midst of incredible pain, Chad and Heidi maintained a positive spirit and held onto their faith in God.

For seven months we continued to hope that this strong young woman would recover from the disease that riddled her body, but she didn't. As Heidi's internal organs began to fail, she lost consciousness and the doctors told Chad that she would not recover.

Chad sent us an e-mail to let us know that Heidi was dying. The e-mail read, "We may have lost the battle, but she has definitely WON the war!" Chad explained what had happened, then wrote, "Although my heart is so very broken and sad, and words cannot express my feelings, I know that Heidi will not suffer any longer and she is most definitely headed for a better place. Heidi and I were both baptized last November and we take great peace in that. So that is why I said we have lost the battle, but definitely won the war."

Just a few hours later, Heidi passed away. Later that night, Chad wrote one more e-mail: "Hello everyone. I will be brief, but I'm writing to let you know that our angel on earth, Heidi, has been called home. She is now at peace. Like so many wonderful things of this earth, they are only here for a short period of time, but the impact left behind echoes beyond the ages."

When life caved in for Chad and Heidi Whitaker, their strong faith in God gave them hope. They didn't just hope that Heidi would recover. To hope in that alone would have been a temporary hope, a false hope, because we *all* will eventually die. But they put their faith and hope in a God who is eternal and who promises, "I am the resurrection and the life. He who believes in me will live, even though he dies" (John 11:25).

Chad said to me at the funeral, "I don't know how people go through this without Christ." We don't always understand God's ways. We wonder how God can use such a tragedy for His good. However, I know that hundreds of people who attended Heidi's funeral and thousands who have heard her story through e-mails, and now through this book, have been inspired by her strong faith in Christ. And we will see Heidi Whitaker again. She may have lost the battle, but she has definitely WON the war. That's faith!

10

JESUS:
When the Road Gets Long,

Faith Perseveres

Hebrews 12:1, 2; Matthew 28:16-20; Acts 1:6-11

Laura Wilkinson had practiced platform diving since she was a little girl. Her lifelong goal was to qualify as a platform diver for the 2000 Olympics in Australia. A few months before the trials, she fell and broke her foot in three places. No one thought she could possibly make the team.

Though she missed seven weeks of training, Laura was determined. She returned to practice with a cast on her foot. The breaks weren't healing properly, but she endured the pain, made it through the qualifying rounds, and was chosen to represent the United States in the Sydney Olympics. Most analysts felt the best she could possibly do was sixth place since other nations are much more proficient in platform diving.

If you watched that drama unfold on television, you know that every time Laura stepped up to the platform, she had a winsome smile on her face and would move her lips. She seemed to be mumbling something to herself, trying to get psyched up for the next dive. She became the darling of the fans.

In an incredibly dramatic finish, Laura came from behind to win the gold medal. She was exuberant. The fans went crazy. In the months that followed, her picture was on Wheaties boxes across the nation and she became an American hero.

We all admire staying power. We admire people with resolve,

people who are determined to reach their goals and aren't easily discouraged. Christopher Columbus, while daring to cross the Atlantic, frequently wrote just four words in his journal to describe the day's events: "Today we sailed on." There are times in our lives when there's no sign of success, but we must keep sailing on. Motivational speaker Paul J. Meyer said, "Ninety percent of those who fail aren't actually defeated—they simply quit."

One of the major problems of our Christian lives is that we quit sailing on. We're not accustomed to sticking with a commitment for very long. When serious temptations come, we give in. If our marriage has a continual stress, we bail out. If Christian leaders disappoint us, we drop out of church. If intellectuals ridicule the Bible, we doubt our faith. If money gets tight, we quit giving. If our attempt to witness is rejected, we clam up. If the nation experiences uncertain times, we get panicky. The people who please God are those who have enough faith to tough it out regardless of the cost.

A man once said to Jesus, "I will follow you wherever you go." Jesus replied, "Foxes have holes and birds of the air have nests, but the Son of Man has no place to lay his head" (Luke 9:57, 58). Jesus urged the man to understand that the Christian life was going to be demanding and he shouldn't follow Him if he wasn't going to follow through.

Jesus said, "No one who puts his hand to the plow and looks back is fit for service in the kingdom of God" (Luke 9:62). Even just an occasional glance over the shoulder harms our Christian influence and self-esteem. He doesn't want us to even glance back wistfully at the past, let alone turn around and return to it. In another passage, Jesus said:

> Suppose one of you wants to build a tower. Will he not first
> sit down and estimate the cost to see if he has enough money
> to complete it? For if he lays the foundation and is not able
> to finish it, everyone who sees it will ridicule him, saying,

"This fellow began to build and was not able to finish" (Luke 14:28-30).

An aborted Christian life gives the enemies of Christ an occasion to ridicule. It discourages other believers and destroys your sense of significance in God's kingdom. But a faithful Christian life is an inspirational witness and a confidence booster. After listing the heroes of the faith, the writer of Hebrews compares the Christian life to a marathon, with those heroes standing along the sidelines and cheering us on:

> Therefore, since we are surrounded by such a great cloud of witnesses, let us throw off everything that hinders and the sin that so easily entangles, and let us run with perseverance the race marked out for us. Let us fix our eyes on Jesus, the author and perfecter of our faith, who for the joy set before him endured the cross, scorning its shame, and sat down at the right hand of the throne of God (Hebrews 12:1, 2).

In a twenty-six-mile marathon, it's not speed but endurance and perseverance that matter. The Christian life is the same. That passage from Hebrews 12 gives us three incentives to persevere when the road gets long.

Be Inspired by the Heroes of the Past

In this book, we've discussed many of the people the author of Hebrews was referring to when he talked about the "great cloud of witnesses" from his previous chapter. We've been encouraged and inspired by their stories. When we consider their shortcomings and their faithfulness throughout adversity, we're motivated to keep going in our own Christian lives.

We can also be inspired to more faithful living by considering the heroes of the faith in our own day. There are many men and women who have persevered through trials and remained faithful, and whose names will some day be listed with the "great cloud of witnesses."

One of my heroes is Ben Merold, who has faithfully preached the gospel all of his life. Ben took a church in Fullerton, California, many years ago that had about 400 members and led it to more than 3,500 members—one of the largest congregations in the country at the time. At age sixty-five, Ben resigned and became the minister of a small congregation in St. Louis with just over 200 members. Five years later, I heard they were averaging nearly 1,000 people in attendance, and the average age of their members was thirty! That church continues to thrive and grow to this day, averaging almost 2,100 people each week with Ben as the minister. He's not quit. He's been faithful to the end.

Another hero of mine is Olin Hay, whose faithfulness has inspired me for years. When Olin first went to college at Cincinnati Bible Seminary, he was a little rough around the edges. A professor once got exasperated with him and commented, "What do they expect me to do when they send me this caliber of a student?" But Olin had a marvelous ministry in Louisville for many years and his ministry had a lasting impact. Olin was the minister who started Southeast Christian Church—my congregation—in 1962.

The week before the new church began, he asked those who were going to help start the new congregation to stand so he could pray for them. Fifty of his members stood. Olin later said his heart sank that day as he looked out and saw some of the church elders, the church organist, the choir director, and his own sister standing! However, he knew he had placed in them a vision for what could happen with this new little church in the suburbs of Louisville. Olin faithfully ministered to that congregation for several more years. He then became the preaching professor at Atlanta Christian College. Even since his retirement, Olin has continued to preach and serve although he is eighty-eight years old.

You know what I appreciate about Olin Hay? He has been an encourager and a supporter to me. He was in an ideal position to criticize, second-guess, and undermine our congregation because of the attention that was being focused on our church, but Olin has been one of my biggest fans in the ministry. I hope I can be as faithful in encouraging my successors as Olin has been to me.

When I am tempted to quit the race, I also think of my parents. My parents are heroes of the faith. They helped start a church in my hometown with thirty people. The church met in an old house and borrowed money on my parents' signature to stay alive. My parents volunteered every weekend at the church. They saw that young congregation go through several incompetent preachers in the early years. Finally, a wonderful preacher began to lead, but he drowned at a Sunday school picnic. The next minister had two little girls who were killed in a freak accident at the state fair. The church went through financial stress, community opposition, weak leadership, terrible sermons, country music (which my mother hates), and yet my parents continued to tithe, pray, serve, and attend every time the doors were open.

Today my home congregation has over two hundred members and is the largest church in the community. Over the years, they've sent more than forty young people into the ministry. As I mentioned earlier, it's no wonder my brother and I have stayed in the ministry for so long. We've been surrounded by a great cloud of witnesses.

Don't forget that there are people who are looking to you for inspiration, too. When you're tempted to quit in the Christian life, make a list of the people who would be hurt by your defection. Ask yourself, "Can I hurt my children, my family, my friends who believe in me? What if they lose heart and follow in my footsteps?" There are people to whom you have been a spiritual leader, so be faithful for their sakes.

Be Prepared for the Inevitable Struggles

Just like a runner training for a race, if you want to persevere in the race of life, you must take the Hebrew writer's advice and do three things.

Eliminate the excess weight

"Let us throw off everything that hinders," he writes (Hebrews 12:1). A man is not going to run a race in an overcoat and combat boots if he can help it. He will make himself as light as possible, throwing off the excess weight that hinders him. In the Christian life, you must discard the things that bog you down. There will be some things that aren't sins but are burdens that weigh you down, which you no longer need to carry and shouldn't if you want to run the best race possible. There might be some old relationships that you must shed. You may have to discard some of your possessions, like Zacchaeus did when he met Jesus, because wealth wrongly earned or too much wealth can be a burden in the race of life. Or you might need to lighten your load by dumping some habits that make you spiritually sluggish and slow you down.

Sidestep the inevitable pitfalls

"Let us throw off . . . the sin that so easily entangles," the Hebrew writer continues. A runner can get entangled along the way. He can step into a pothole, trip on another runner, or make a wrong turn. In the race of life, sin can entangle and overcome us.

A man starts out buying a pornographic magazine when he's out of town on a business trip. At first it seems harmless. But there is a law of sin—it's like a drug that creates an increased appetite and diminishing returns. Within a few months, it's an X-rated movie in the hotel room, then visits to nude bars, and then prostitution and ruination. His mind is polluted, his reputation is ruined, and his family is in shambles. Sin has entangled and overcome him.

A woman starts out embellishing a story to make it more interesting. Then she lies to cover up her first lie and repeats her lies till she believes them herself. Eventually, she is so entangled in lies that she is incapable of telling the truth. Her credibility is lost, her relationships are destroyed, and her witness is negated. Sin has entangled her.

If you are to persevere in the Christian life, you can't let sin deceive and entangle you.

Pace yourself for the long haul

"Let us run with perseverance the race marked out for us," writes the author of Hebrews.

One of our elders, Mount Davis, has participated in four Boston Marathons. I asked him why he went through the rigid three months of training and punished himself to run in a twenty-six-mile race. He said, "It's not to win. There are twenty thousand people who participate in that race. Only fifty of them have a legitimate chance of winning. The goal is not to finish first but to finish as fast as you can. There's a certain satisfaction that comes from finishing to the best of your capabilities. The fun is the challenge."

Start out at a steady pace. Mount said, "When you first start the race, you're pumped up and feel so good you're tempted to sprint too fast. Too much speed is a liability. You have to force yourself to run at a steady pace. A general rule is, 'If it feels good, slow down. If it feels bad, speed up.'"

Some Christians need to hear that advice. There are some who get so excited when they first come to Christ that they jump into every possible service opportunity, Bible study, and worship experience. Within a year, when the newness wears off or they're exhausted, burnout sets in. Unless they find something even more exciting, they get discouraged. There has to be a sort of spiritual pacing. You can't attend every class, play on the ball team, work in the nursery, be a small group leader, and sing in the choir all at the same time.

Heb. 13:1-8

Persevere when you near the end. Mount Davis described "hitting the wall" in a marathon:

> About twenty-two miles into the race, you really have to battle discouragement. They call it "hitting the wall." In the Boston Marathon, at the twenty-two-mile marker, you go up Heartbreak Hill. At the top of the hill there is a policeman in a cherry picker who announces, "You just ran Heartbreak Hill. It's all downhill from here." That sounds good, but you look out and there's another hill in your vision. The last four miles do descend a little, but the overall race still has ups and downs. You're exhausted, and those last four miles are very difficult.

One of the real barriers in the Christian life is discouragement in the later years. People disappoint you. You disagree with decisions that the church leaders have made. You "hit the wall" because your energy is low. You have to work through your times of discouragement and hang on.

"[Don't] grow weary and lose heart," the Hebrew writer challenged (Hebrews 12:3). The Christian life is a long, grueling race. You have to run smart and run with perseverance. In the end, there is the satisfaction of knowing you did the best you could with what God gave you, and you can look forward to hearing the Lord say, "Well done, good and faithful servant." John Maxwell said, "Life is a grindstone. Whether it grinds you down or polishes you up depends on what you're made of."

Be Focused on the Person of Jesus Christ

Let us fix our eyes on Jesus, the author and perfecter of our faith, who for the joy set before him endured the cross, scorning its shame, and sat down at the right hand of the throne of God. Consider him who endured such opposition from sinful men, so that you will not grow weary and lose heart (Hebrews 12:2, 3).

Consider the perseverance of Jesus. He resisted fierce temptation. Satan came to Him with appealing offers of pleasure, popu-
larity, and power, but Jesus was without sin—He refused to get
entangled in Satan's trap.

He also endured intense opposition. His enemies ridiculed
Him, criticized Him, alienated Him, and lied about Him. Yet
Jesus kept persevering; He stayed the course. And He did so with a
spirit of joy. In the passage above we read, ". . . for the *joy* set
before him [he] endured the cross."

Jesus is the author and perfecter of our faith. He's not only the
one who started our faith by dying on the cross for us, He's also
the one who stays with us in the faith, boosting us up by His
Spirit when we struggle. And He's the one who will finish our
faith when we stand before Him on Judgment Day and say,
"Forgiven! Not guilty!"

When you are tempted to quit, waiver, or look back, fix your
eyes on Jesus. Don't look at people; they'll let you down. Don't
look at the church or its leaders; they are imperfect. Don't focus
on yourself or you'll really be disappointed. Look to Christ. He
never disappoints, He is faithful, and He promises to reward you
in the end.

After Laura Wilkinson won the gold medal, reporter Andrea
Joyce interviewed her and said, "It's been thirty-six years since the
United States won a gold medal in platform diving. Can you put
your emotions into words?" Laura immediately said, "I can do all
things through Christ who strengthens me." Then it was learned
that each time she walked to the end of the platform, she was not
chanting or mumbling to psyche herself up before she dove; she
was repeating her favorite verse of Scripture from Philippians 4:13.
She later told *World* magazine, "That's always been a favorite verse
of mine, but this time it really meant something. It became real. I
really was trying to do something that I can't do. God was with
me."[30] That's faith!

When you are facing trials that threaten to discourage you,

such as physical ailments, emotional stress, family pressures, or financial difficulties, sail on. Stay the course with resolution. Fight through "the wall." Don't quit. Pray this prayer: "Lord, help me stand, not fall; lift, not let down; be true, not false; courageous, not afraid. And just when I'm tempted to fold, please bring to my mind the memory of Jesus who stood alone and stayed courageous and went all the way to the cross for me." Have faith in Christ. Then, when you have persevered, you can say with Paul,

> I have fought the good fight, I have finished the race, I have kept the faith. Now there is in store for me the crown of righteousness, which the Lord, the righteous Judge, will award to me on that day—and not only to me, but also to all who have longed for his appearing (2 Timothy 4:7, 8).

ENDNOTES

[1]Max Lucado, *No Wonder They Call Him the Savior* (Sisters, Oregon: Multnomah, 1986), pp. 117, 119.

[2]Paul G. Stoltz, Ph.D., *Adversity Quotient: Turning Obstacles Into Opportunities* (New York: John Wiley & Sons, Inc., 1997), pp. 5-6. Reprinted by permission of John Wiley & Sons, Inc.

[3]*Ibid.*, pp. 11-12.

[4]*Ibid.*, p. 18.

[5]*Ibid.*, pp. 14-15, 22.

[6]*Ibid.*, p. 5.

[7]*Ibid.*, pp. 32-35.

[8]James Dobson, Ph.D. *What Wives Wish Their Husbands Knew About Women* (Wheaton, Illinois: Tyndale House Publishers, 1975), pp. 22-23.

[9]Josh McDowell, source unknown. Bob Russell first mentioned this quote from Mr. McDowell in a sermon many years ago and the original source has long since been misplaced. Our apologies to Mr. McDowell.

[10]©1984 Cook Communications Ministries. *Healing for Damaged Emotions* by David Seamands. Copied with permission. May not be further reproduced. All rights reserved.

[11]*Ibid.*, pp. 49-56.

[12]*Ibid.*, p. 53.

[13]Elmer Towns, source unknown.

[14]Joel C. Gregory, *Growing Pains of the Soul* (Waco, Texas: Word, Inc., 1987), p. 140.

[15]Steve Saint, "Did They Have to Die?" *Christianity Today*, September 16, 1996. Archived at *christianitytoday.com/ct/6ta/6ta020.html*.

[16] *Ibid.*

[17] S.I. McMillen, M.D., *None of These Diseases* (Westwood, New Jersey: Spire Books, 1963), pp. 7-158.

[18] "Rock of Ages." Words by Augustus M. Toplady; music by Thomas Hastings. Public domain.

[19] Norman Lear, *Leadership Magazine*, p. 64.

[20] J. Oswald Sanders, *Spiritual Manpower* (Chicago: Moody Press, 1965), p. 105.

[21] *Ibid.*, p. 102.

[22] Julie Connelly, "The Trophy Wife Is Back With Brains," *Fortune*, April 3, 1995, p. 102.

[23] J. Oswald Sanders, *ibid.*, p. 106.

[24] Steve Chapman, *A Look at Life From a Deer Stand* (Madison, Tennessee: Pleasant View Press, 1996), pp. 65-67.

[25] This is a true story but Annie is not my friend's real name.

[26] Patricia Klein, et. al., *Growing Up Born Again: A Whimsical Look at the Blessings and Tribulations of Growing Up Born Again* (Old Tappan, New Jersey: Fleming H. Revell Co., 1987), p. 22.

[27] Harold Bloom, "Heroes and Icons," *Time*, Vol. 153, No. 23, June 14, 1999.

[28] "Robert Pershing Wadlow—Alton's Gentle Giant," Alton Museum of History and Art Web site, *altonweb.com.*

[29] Ross Brodfuehrer, devotion, *The Southeast Lookout*, Louisville, Kentucky, September 2, 1999.

[30] "Wilkinson: God Was With Me," *World,* Vol. 15, No. 51, December 30, 2000 –January 6, 2001. Archived at *worldmag.com/world/issue /12-30-00/national_3.asp.*